on
BEDFORD
AT WAR

Published by
KELSEY PUBLISHING LTD

Printed in Singapore by Stamford Press PTE Ltd.
on behalf of
Kelsey Publishing Ltd,
Cudham Tithe Barn,
Berry's Hill,
Cudham,
Kent TN16 3AG
Tel: 01959 541444
Fax: 01959 541400
E-mail: kelseybooks@kelsey.co.uk
Website: www.kelsey.co.uk
www.cmvmag.co.uk

ISBN 1 873098 72 3

Acknowledgements:
Robert Coates, Brian Veale, Pat Ware

INTRODUCTION

This book, which is largely the work of long-time Bedford fan and keen historian, Robert Coates, has been compiled from articles which have appeared in Classic Military Vehicle over the last four years.

The book tells the story of what was perhaps Britain's only truly 'classic' military vehicle – the once-ubiquitous Bedford.

The story starts with the company's Genesis, in 1931, to its effective Exodus, in 1986 and covers virtually every military product which the company produced. From the early vans and lorries of the 'thirties, through the O series and the truly iconic MW and QL trucks of WW2, to the magnificent achievement of the Churchill infantry tank. Post-war military products included the still-born FV1300 project, the RL workhorses – and the Green Goddesses, the MK/MJ, and the TM4-4 and 6-6 which serve to this day – not forgetting the Vauxhall staff cars of the early thirties.

In its 55-year life, Bedford supplied, literally, hundreds of thousands of vehicles both to the British armed forces and to many countries overseas.

After two valiant attempts at revival, Bedford finally succumbed to world market pressures in the late 'eighties, but the company's heyday slogan, 'You see them everywhere', remained true for many years: look at any old photos or film of the period, featuring military operations or civilian traffic and you are almost certain to see a Bedford.

Perhaps this book should be dedicated to the millions of people who have been involved in the design, building, ownership, operation, driving, maintenance, restoration, care and admiration of what must be the best known and most numerous of all British commercial vehicles – the Bedford!

Pat Ware
Editor, Classic Military Vehicle

CONTENTS

The Bedford Story:

BEDFORD

In the first part of a new series, Robert Coates asks if Bedford was *the* Classic Military Vehicle of all time?

Bedfords formed the backbone of the British Army's vehicle fleet for well over 60 years. Even before 1931, the year that Bedford was set up, Vauxhall Motors, their parent company, had been major suppliers of staff cars to the Army and a very brief look at what is probably the best known of these may be of interest before trying to answer the question of whether Bedford can claim to be the classic - British - military vehicle of all time.

It was a 'D type' which carried General Allenby on his victory ride into Jerusalem: another was the first car to cross the Rhine into Germany after the 1918 Armistice. Production for civilian customers continued until 1922 with the 'D type' developing into the Model 30/98. A few of these were supplied, but only to 'top brass', mainly because of their colossal price-tag. The 30/98 had a 100bhp, 23.8 RAC horsepower engine of 4.25 litres capacity and was capable of 'a guaranteed 100 mph' and, although only some 600 or so were built, over 170 still survive.

Vauxhall were still supplying cars to the Army in the period just before and during WW2 as, of course, were other suppliers, notably Austin, Hillman, Standard and Humber.

Smallest in the range was the 10hp 'H type', which was introduced in 1937. In its civilian guise, this was one of the most successful cars of its period. The standard four-door, four-seater saloon cost only £168 and its four-cylinder, 1200cc engine enabled it to cover 42 miles on a gallon of petrol - or so Vauxhall said. The 'H type' was the first British car built using the integral body-chassis method and more than 10,000 were sold in the first five months following its introduction. It was joined later by the much larger Vauxhall 14 and the 'intermediate' 12/4, in which this writer ostensibly learned to drive. 'Ostensibly' because, having had a school-holiday job as second man on a furniture

Left: The 1914-18 Vauxhall 'D type' army staff car. This beautiful vehicle now forms part of the Vauxhall Veteran Vehicle Fleet - their 'Heritage Collection' - from whose brochure this picture is reproduced with their kind permission.

Below: The 1937 Vauxhall 10/4 'H type' saloon was used as a staff car, suitably camouflaged and fitted with 'blackout' lamp covers. This one is also part of Vauxhall's 'Heritage Collection'.

Nearly 2000 Vauxhall 'D type' Army staff cars were supplied to the War Office during the Great War. The 'D type' was a development of the earlier, and probably more famous, 'Prince Henry' Vauxhall of the 1911-14 era - a car which was frequently used in racing and speed trials. It had a four-cylinder engine of just under four-litres capacity and was rated at 25 RAC horsepower - a measure which had little to do with its power and everything to do with its dimensions. This handsome beast, weighing in at over a ton-and-a-half, saw wartime service in many theatres, including Egypt and Salonika, and earned itself the epithet of being 'the finest car on active service'. 'In the opinion of experts,' proclaimed a contemporary advertisement, 'no car has gained such credit in military service'.

Above: This photo, of a Vauxhall 30/98 dating from 1926, was taken some years ago at the Prescott Hill Climb. Someone must have paid a fortune for that number-plate but well worth it on what must be one of the most desirable of vintage cars!

delivery van, learning to drive was something which had taken place long before the statutory 17th birthday - even taking out laden vans solo when the regular driver failed to turn up. From the first lesson, my father was astonished at what a good teacher he was, even managing to instruct quite passable double de-clutch gear-changes from the onset!

The Bedford story is, however, not about staff cars but about 'army lorries' and, although many would think, the military story starts with the 15cwt MW 'pneumonia wagon', Bedford lorries were in use by the armed forces well before the MW became commonplace. Many hundreds of civilian two- and three-tonners were impressed, requisitioned, commandeered - call it what you will - during September 1939 upon the outbreak of war.

Requisitioning started in sensible numbers from 1 September 1939 but gathered pace rapidly. New cars and motor-cycles were impressed direct from the manufacturers and distributors; lorries, from wherever they could find them, many having been previously ear-marked. In the nine days following 2 September, extra staff had to be taken on to deal with the rush and, a 'mid-stream' system change meant that much in the way of useful statistics was lost. However, 'impressment' continued at the rate of about 1200 vehicles per day during this early part of September. The records do not show exactly what they were - only for what they were to be used.

A typical account of how civilian vehicles were pressed into service is told by Howard Hunt, a long-time Bedford enthusiast and a schoolboy at the time. In the summer holidays of 1939, a

representative from the War Office arrived to inspect and value his father's two-year old 'W type'. The sum of £130 was offered and accepted as being near enough to market value and a travel warrant was issued for the return journey from Aldershot, where the vehicle had to be presented by 2.30pm the following day. All tools and 'extras' had to be removed and, when the driver returned, he recounted how there had been hundreds of other vehicles at the depot, all of which were to be sprayed khaki that day for delivery to France within 24 hours.

Most of the Bedfords which were requisitioned would have been 'W types' of one sort or another since the K, M, and O models were only announced in 1938 and, whilst they sold well, few were around by September 1939, so few were available to be impressed.

Many hundreds of impressed vehicles were abandoned at Dunkirk including hundreds of Bedford 'W types', and this story begins with these early Bedford models.

The very earliest Bedfords, designated 'W type', were for 30cwt to two-ton payloads. They entered a marketplace dominated, at one end, by Austin, Ford and Morris who turned out trucks based on the heaviest of the cars in their range whilst, at the other end of the weight range were the 'heavies', dominated by AEC, Foden, Leyland and Scammell. These were all capable of carrying loads of five tons and over - although a vehicle's payload capacity was, in the 'thirties, decidedly 'nominal'. In later years, Bedford even advertised that their vehicles were quite adequate for a 50% overload!

Fitted with a six-cylinder, 26.33 RAC horsepower engine which developed 44bhp, the Bedford's performance

Above: Next month we'll start to look at the wartime Bedfords, like the ubiquitous 'MW'.

Bedford production, lorries, vans and buses: 1931-39

These production figures, for Bedford's first 10 years, are extracted from Vauxhall's Engineering Records Department (ERD). The production year ran from 1 October to 30 September so 1939 includes no wartime production.

1931	11,487	1932	10,529
1933	15,173	1934	17,823
1935	23,741	1936	26,210
1937	31,783	1938	27,474
1939	18,185		

The breakdown for 1939 was 14,402 examples of the 'W type', 856 'ASYC' and 'AXYC' vans, 1066 'BYC' and 'BXC' vans, and 1861 'HC' vans. Numbers of any of these will have found their way into military service.

was very smooth, especially when compared with some of the four-cylinder offerings which were around. Inevitably, comparisons were made with the Vauxhall-assembled Chevrolet, which the Bedfords replaced. Bedford believed that the 'W type' was better than the Chevrolet - one example of this was in the use of a four-speed gearbox, compared with the American's three-speeder. Both 'boxes were, of course, of the 'crash' type, a feature which was retained in Bedfords until after the War, even though Vauxhall cars were amongst the first to be fitted with synchromesh. The Bedford gearbox also had four main bearings for their mainshafts, a feature which helped to give them their distinctive sound, although there were several other factors, too. The distinctive sound of the Bedford is something which remains one of its most endearing characteristics.

As for the engine, Bedfords had full-pressure lubrication whilst the Chevrolets had to make do with the - rather old-fashioned, by 1931 - splash lubrication. With a cylinder bore of $3^5/_{16}$in and a

stroke of $3^3/_4$in giving 3177cc, the Bedford engine was a described as a long-stroke unit, ie the stroke is greater than the cylinder bore. The longer 'throw' of the crankshaft gave a nice, 'torquey', engine which required fewer gear-changes than its short-stroke counterpart, (the 'over-square' engine) which, with the ratios reversed, requires revs to be kept higher to develop power. Other features of the 'W types' were their 6V coil ignition, a pedal-operated starter and rod-operated mechanical brakes operating on all four wheels.

The real breakthrough came with the Stepney-Acres designed 'model WT' three-tonners which were first seen at the Motor Show in November 1933. The main feature was that the engine had been moved forward so that its centre-line lay directly over the front axle - an innovation which not only gave a shorter bonnet but was also better for load distribution, setting the standard for all light commercials for many years to come. It was supplied with an uprated engine - from 44bhp to 57bhp which, in turn, was later uprated again to 64bhp by adding an improved down-draught carburettor. Fitted with vacuum servo brakes and with an unladen weight of less than 2½ tons, they could travel at speeds up to the 30mph limit - although, for vehicles over 2½ tons unladen the speed limit was still 20mph.

By 1935, Bedford was actively co-operating with the War Department, but more of that in a future article. Next month we shall start looking at vehicles which were supplied direct to the War Office starting with the ubiquitous 'K', 'M' and 'O types'.

Left: A line-up of 1930s Bedfords at a meeting of Vauxhall Owners' clubs at Billing Aquadrome, near Northampton. These three models, the 'WLG' three-tonner of about 1935, the 'WT' three-tonner of 1936 and the early 'O-type' with its one-piece windscreen, dating from 1938, are typical of the sort of vehicles which would have been called up in September 1939 - and abandoned at Dunkirk.

BEDFORD'S PRE-WAR MODELS

The second instalment of Robert Coates' superb series on Bedford military vehicles

Last month, Robert started with the creation of the company in 1931 and brought us to the outbreak of War in 1939. This month we take a look at those models supplied directly to the War Department.

From their inception in 1931, Bedford introduced annual improvements to their lorries, usually in time to be announced at the Motor Shows at Earls Court. By late 1935, the whole range had received a face-lift which included a wheelbase reduction from 157in to 143in. Both of these dimensions would have later relevance to the 3-ton military models - the 4x2 'Model OY' and the 4x4 'Model QL', respectively.

On 8 July 1938, Bedford announced that their 'W Series' 3-tonners were to be replaced by the K, M and O range, first appearing on the roads in 1939. Production continued until 6 February 1940 when it was suspended for war-time vehicle building, resuming once hostilities were over.

Just prior to this, in the early summer of 1938, a new engine had been made available for the WT models and this was fitted as standard to the new range and to all war-time production, becoming the standard Bedford six-cylinder 'WD' engine with an output of 27.34 RAC-horsepower. Perhaps the War Department, intent on as much standardisation as possible, took things a little too far in this case as the same engine was fitted to the 15-cwt MW as the 6-ton articulated, off-road QL.

Bedford's war-time models were all based on this new range. Being relatively cheap, very robust, simple to drive and simple to maintain, it was no accident that the War Department chose Bedford as one of the main suppliers of vehicles in the 'up to three ton' category. 'You see them everywhere' said the advert and, indeed, you did. But it was not just the military, 'ruggedised', models which found their way into War Department fleets. There was also a requirement for ordinary, road-going lorries of various types and for chassis with 'special' bodies such as ambulances and tankers which could use the standard offering.

It is difficult to ascertain precise numbers built of each model because chassis numbers were, initially, allocated

Above: This model MSC, restored in RAF livery, is typical of the small general-purpose lorries supplied by Bedford up to 1940. Photographed in 1998 at the Yeovil Festival of Transport.

Right: A contemporary advert for the 'model OSA' articulated tractor unit which was used by the Army with a drop-side Scammell trailer for 6-ton general-service duties.

as a group across all three models, K, M and O. However, a total of 9856 vehicles left the factory in 1939-40 and, in 1945, when production was resumed, only 52 were added to the total. These last few may have been for civilian use but the vast majority produced between 1940 and 1945 were for the Armed Forces supplied under contract to the Ministry of War Transport (MoWT).

By 1946 production was again in full swing and over 25,000 were produced - a figure which went on increasing year by year until the early 'fifties.

Taking each of the new, 'civilian'

models in turn, the 'K type', or 'Model K', as it was sometimes known, was for a payload of 30cwt on a 120in wheelbase. For military use, the 'K type', lorry 30/40 cwt' was produced with a

canvas tilt body; it ran 32x6 tyres, single at the rear, one of the features which makes it easy to identify, with disc wheels all round.

The 'M type' was for operation at 2 tons but was frequently used for loads well in excess of this. As a result it was often referred to, even in official documents, as the '2-3 tonner'. Both the 'K type' and the 'M type' had longer bonnets than the 'O type', thus obviating the need for the engine to intrude into the cab. There were two basic models, the ML (long), with a 143in wheelbase and the MS (short), at 120in. The ML models consisted, in standard form, of the 2-3 ton lorry with a tilt body and heavy-duty 32x6 tyres, dualled at the rear. The standard

version had a drop-side body and, apart from an additional row of cooling louvres on the bonnet and its canvas tilt, was indistinguishable from the civilian truck.

There were also three 'ML modified' models. The first was a four compartment, 800-gallon petrol tanker with a tank supplied by Aluminium Plant & Vessel. The chassis specification was standard except for an external screen running the full depth of the cab behind the driver which prevented heat and sparks from the engine - and perhaps even cigarette ends - coming anywhere near the load. The exhaust pipe was also re-routed to exit ahead of the screen and the electrics were changed to a two-wire system. In 1939-40, 45 of these ML55 2-ton long-wheelbase tankers were supplied to the MoWT.

Next was an ambulance with a Mann Egerton body, a total of 397 of these being supplied. Internally, the layout gave the option of four stretchers plus attendant or 10 'sitting cases'. The cab had no doors or, at best, canvas ones (as on the 'Number 2 body Mk 1L') and there was a communicating door between the cab and the body with double swing-doors and a folding step at the rear. Overall, the ML ambulance was similar in appearance to Austin's Model K2Y - the standard 2-ton ambulance, made famous in the film 'Ice Cold in Alex'.

Bedford and Austin ambulances had many similarities in appearance and 'spotters' can easily be confused by both having the same, WD specification body - right down to the Red Cross markings and details of the ventilators in the body sides - referred to as 'air conditioning' in the official specification! However, the Austin was slightly shorter, on a 134in wheelbase and some were fitted with rotary ventilators in the roof, a feature for which no evidence can be found on the Bedford chassis. Both ran 10.50x16 tyres, single at the rear.

The Bedford OSA articulated tractor unit, as supplied on some early contracts. The domestic appliance trailer is unlikely to have found a military application.

A 2-3 ton end-tipper was also available on the 'ML modified' chassis. The body, with 18in drop-sides, was built and fitted by Spurling's who also installed the hand-operated Clayton-Dewandre tipping gear. Unusually, whilst retaining single tyres on the rear, those fitted at the front were of a different size - 7.00x20 on the front, 7.00x34 on the rear. Only one spare was carried - for the rear wheels - and it does not take much imagination to work out whose law applies when punctures were experienced!

There were also three models produced on the MS, short-wheelbase, chassis. The 'tender (RAF)', which was similar to the 'K type' with a tilt body built by Spurling, and with payload restricted to 30-cwt. Designated MSC, it was used by the RAF as a general 'fetch and carry' vehicle, often ferrying crews to their aircraft rather than using the purpose-built coaches. Identifying points - apart from the disc wheels on the K type - were the rear wings which were rounded on the K type but of a more military design - a flat metal panel with a suspended flexible flap behind the rear wheel on the MSC. More straightforward identification would have been the blue paint and RAF markings! For some unknown reason, this model had different tyres from the others: 10.50x16 whilst the others had 32x6.

The two other MS models were both 2-3 ton tippers. One had three-way, hydraulic tipping gear by Bromilow and Edwards; the other, an end-tipper, had a Spurling body and hand-operated Spenborough tipping mechanism. Both ran on dual rear tyres and both had similar body measurements, the three-way tipper having a slightly wider body.

Virtually any armoured vehicle built on a commercial chassis was called an Armadillo and they appeared on many chassis, including Bedford 'W types', but the MLD version seems to come in for special mention together with the

Right: Bedford 'ML' type 115 Mk 1 radio vehicle. A prime example of the 'non-ruggedised' lorries supplied for the war effort by Bedford (illustration extracted from official wartime publication (AP 2276J) and is reproduced by kind permission of the MVT).

Above: Long wheelbase 'M type' 2-3 tonners also had the 'long' bonnet, and a divided windscreen.

Below: A 'K type' 30-cwt fitted with a Spurling's 'Spurmobus'(!) passenger body. Note the long bonnet and disc wheels - features of the 'K type'.

OYD. Two versions of the MLD were made - Mark 1 and Mark 2 - the latter having a larger armoured 'box' and better armour protection at the front including an armoured screen with a vision slot for the driver. The cab had armoured doors, fixed shut on the passenger side but with a vision slot. The enclosed 'hut' on the back was accessed through a sliding iron door.

Largest of the K, M, O, range was, possibly, the most evocative Bedford of all time - the 'O type'. Its era was a very long one - introduced in 1938 and continuing in production until 1953. But, after the War, vehicles had to be made to last and many 'O types' were still working hard for a living well into the 'sixties and beyond.

The 'O type' had a shorter bonnet than its stablemates, the

engine thus protruded into the cab, and the front wheel arch into the outline of the cab door. It was available with two wheelbases, in standard and uprated form. The standard 3-ton long wheelbase versions were the OL (157in) and the OS (111in). These became, in uprated form, Models OL40 and OS40, both being 5-tonners. Supplied to the Army, they were simply designated OS and OL, rated for 3-4 ton working, and there were three models, one 'long' and two 'short'. The long-wheelbase 'lorry, 3-4 ton', was a standard, open, two-part-dropside lorry with a centre stanchion midway along the length; these ran on heavy duty 32x6 tyres. Of the two OS models, one was a 3-4 ton, three-way tipper with Bromilow and Edwards hydraulic tipping gear. The other was an articulated tractor unit with a Scammell-built trailer and body, for operation at 6-ton payload.

At roughly the same time as Bedford announced their K, M, O Range, Austin announced a very similar looking truck in the 2-3 ton category - so similar, in fact, that it was frequently described, much to Austin's chagrin, as 'the Birmingham Bedford'. This, too was supplied to the War Department in large numbers, notably as an ambulance.

Normal production of Bedfords resumed in 1945 by which time they had supplied over 250,000 lorries for the war effort.

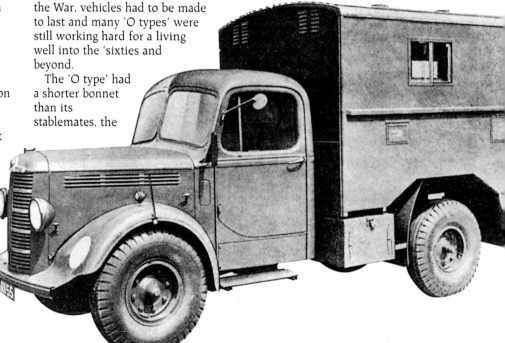

BEDFORD'S Pneumonia Waggon

In the third instalment of Robert Coates' superb series on Bedford military vehicles, we take a look at one of the definitive WW2 Bedfords - the MW.

The two predominant 4x2 models built by Bedford during WW2 were the 15-cwt MW and the 3-ton OY, both having specifications similar to their pre-war civilian counterparts. Some technical details were different - Solex carburettors and 12V electrics on the military vehicles, Zenith carburettors and 6V on the civilians - but the biggest difference was in their appearance. Gone were the elegant, nicely-rounded bonnet and chromed grille strips. In their place were flat sheets of metal which looked as if they had been cobbled together - and, in a sense, they had.

BEDFORD had taken part in military trials since 1935 working to a WD specification issued in 1933 but, by 1939, had only successfully developed one vehicle. The prototype, designated WD1 by Vauxhall - and eventually allocated census number Z3810602 - had had its military content increased gradually. It was based on the then current 2-3 tonner but had larger tyres, an improved cooling system, and a chassis modified to improve ground clearance. The eventual production model, although based on the 1937 prototype, utilised the newly-announced (1938) M-type chassis.

During the trials, so the story goes, it was decided to fit a larger air-cleaner suitable for operations in the desert. However, there was no room for it so the bonnet had to be widened and, hurriedly, fronted up with a flat metal sheet and a mesh grille, topped off by a hinged flat 'lid' - flatter on the prototype than on the eventual production model. It has to be said that the whole visual effect was very functional as well as supposedly facilitating de-contamination from gas attack. Access for maintenance was easy; if the panels were damaged they could be repaired much more readily and they looked right for a military vehicle. Later, it was decided to revert to the original air-cleaner but the authorities liked the chunky version, and it stayed. Later models had changes made to the radiator grill, brushguard and bonnet sides but the basic shape remained unchanged.

Designated MW, this was the smallest wartime Bedford - a model on which many new drivers cut their teeth. It was geared, governed and carburetted slightly differently from the larger models but was, nevertheless, quite a flyer - the 28 RAC-horsepower Bedford engine generated 72bhp, giving a massive 22bhp per ton with a laden GS cargo body. The legal minimum horsepower for

Canvas doors, fly-screens and a circular Bedford badge mark this as a pre-production specimen. Steel doors and a full-width divided 'screen adorned later models.

commercial vehicles was, and still is, 6 bhp/ton and, in those days and for some time afterwards, trucks were considered high-powered if they could boast 10!

The four-speed gearbox gave the MW a theoretical top speed of 40mph at a governed 2425rpm, though it seemed a lot faster. Final drive was spiral bevel through fully-floating axles; suspension was by semi-elliptic leaf springs with hydraulic shock absorbers all round. The Lockheed hydraulic foot-brake acted on all four wheels but, with no servo,

This handsomely - restored MWD GS, belonging to Roger Dyer, is seen here at the 1999 Festival of Transport at Yeovil, Somerset.

braking power was directly proportionate to pedal pressure which, bearing in mind the strange driving position was not always a lot! The mechanical handbrake acted on the rear wheels only. Tyres were 9.00x16 and the vehicle could turn in a 44-foot circle. A 20-gallon fuel tank gave an operating radius of about 230-240 miles depending upon where, how and by whom it was driven!

The cab had a canvas hood and no doors - a simple chain or a canvas flap fulfilled that role - and the MW was widely known as the 'pneumonia waggon'. It was not uncommon for occupants to pull the hood down to the top of the tiny aero-screens to try to keep out the cold. Being of the 'normal control' type, there wasn't even much engine-heat in the cab to improve driving conditions.

The front track was wider than that at the rear. This mattered little as the MW was not really intended for any serious off-road work, even though it could be quite handy until the going became really rugged - when a four-wheel drive vehicle would have been required. Its ground clearance was respectable even for an off-roader, with 9in under the axle and 16in under the belly.

From the visual identification viewpoint, there really should be no confusion between the MW and the 30cwt OX yet some so-called 'reference' books are clearly confused, showing the

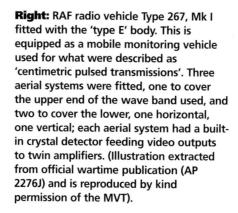

Arlington converted scores of MWs to forward control for delivery work - the radiator is rather 'Jensen' like. This example also seen at Billing Aquadrome.

OX mobile canteen - a standard body on the OX chassis - as an MW, whilst referring to it as a mobile tea-van! The MW had a 99in wheelbase - the OX was 111in, and was usually equipped with much 'fatter' tyres (32x6 or 10.50x16 on the OX; 9.00x16 on the MW). Additionally, the MW body was just under 78in wide internally, compared with the mobile canteen's 102in.

Right at the beginning of the War, Bedford received an order for 50 'small, utility vehicles' fitted with anti-tank guns. Amazingly, these were delivered within seven days, a feat which earned Bedford a repeat order for 27,000 vehicles! Of these, 11,000 were MWs, 5,000 were 30-cwt OXs and 11,000 were 3-ton OYs. The table shows the numbers of MWs produced in each year of the war.

The 'standard' MW was the MWD 'general service' of which there were many derivatives. Early models had an open driving compartment with seating for a driver and one passenger. It had a folding detachable canvas top, and an open body with fixed sides and tailboard and fittings for a canvas top or tilt. From 1943 the cab was enclosed and provided with half-doors and detachable side curtains, and the windscreen was changed from aero-screens to a full-width, flat, divided screen with two wipers - a luxury for its time.

MWCs were supplied in chassis-cab form and a variety of bodies were fitted. The MWC water bowser had an oval-shaped, 200-gallon tank which was modified on later versions to have flat sides. A pump was fitted at the front intended to pick up water 'from any

Rather heavily over-restored, but nevertheless in beautiful condition, this pair of MWs was on show at the Bedford gathering at Billing Aquadrome in 1993.

Above: Ready to leave the Luton factory is this batch of MWs surrounded by various 'civilian' models and a column of 3-ton OYs.

Production of Bedford Model MW: 1940-45

Year	ERD* total	Chassis numbers: start	finish	total	Engine numbers: start	finish	total
1940	14,440	1001	18,750	17,750	2001	17,447	15,747
1941	13,965	18,751	33,719	14,969	17,448	32,258	14,811
1942	13,746	33,720	46,021	12,302	32,259	46,136	13,878
1943	14,666	46,022	55,885	9864	46,137	57,188	11,052
1944	4270	55,886	64,484	8599	57,189	67,391	10,203
1945	4908	64,485	66,995	2511	67,392	72,506	5115
Total	65,995			65,995			70,806

* Engineering Records Department, Vauxhall Motors, 1949

Numbers of vehicles and engines do not tally because nearly 5000 'spare' engines were produced; annual figures based on chassis numbers disagree with ERD totals due to differences in timing between allocation and production.

Left: Very tidy MWC restored with the 1944 markings of the RAF Regiment and described by its owner as 'very original'. Delivered as part of contract S5799, the RAF number is confirmed by the contract plate riveted to the interior. Any further information would be most welcome.

Above: Restored as an MWD, this MWC was originally in service with the Royal navy. It's wartime registration was 70257RN and it was renumbered in 1949 as 85RN55. It was sold at auction at Ruddington in 1958 and the new owner removed the body to allow conversion to a light breakdown/recovery vehicle....

...the body has subsequently been traced and is doing sterling service as a paint store.

available source'; on early models it was driven by the starter-dog, on later types, it was driven by a gearbox power take-off. In addition to the pick-up pump, there were two hand-operated pumps. All water was filtered and chlorinated, and purifying tablets were included in the tool-kit.

The MWG anti-aircraft variant was, largely taken up by the RAF. It had a platform body equipped with an octagonal base plate and clamping brackets to take either the latest universal mounting, developed by Vauxhall, or a Hazard Baird mounting for a 20mm gun. Some models had a 20mm Oerlikon, others the Polsten which was developed to supplement the Oerlikon and had its

Right: Posing, or practising? Either way this MWD is showing off its wading abilities, no doubt with the engine suitably waterproofed which, on this occasion, it doesn't seem to need.

own mounting. The gun was loaded on the vehicle by a small hand-winch up tubular ramps. A locker at the front held four 60-round circular magazines or eight 20-round Polsten magazines.

The MWT anti-tank tractor/portee had a very similar body to the GS version but with a detachable cover and superstructure, and seats for personnel. Gun-loading ramps were carried in outrigger brackets on either side of the body and the gun-wheels rested in curved channels in a fixed ramp on the floor. Armament consisted, usually, of a 2-pounder but early versions had the 1914-vintage Hotchkiss machine gun.

Several variants, and sub-variants of the MWR radio van were available, records being confused by referring both to the body type and to the signals set installed.

Some had rigid body sides; others, like the MWR FFW ('fitted for wireless') had wooden sides with a tilt. Wireless, incidentally, usually denoted Morse code; radio referred to 'voice' communication.

There was also a slightly modified version, preferred by the RAF, known as MWV. Their MWV 'E' Type, for example, was a wireless shell adapted from the MWR, retaining the enclosed van-type radio body but itself having 'subtypes'; eg, signals 107, 108, 314, 315, and 316 bodies. The MWV is distinguishable from the MWR by its wheel arches, constructed to give a 'general purpose' body fitting suitable also for the Commer Q2/Q15 or CMP Ford F15.

Several other versions were available including 'machy' and 'machy K' the latter carrying a Murex arc-welding set.

Competition for the MW came from many sources, including Austin with their old-fashioned taxi-cab based BYD; the Commer Beetle, Q2 and Q15; Ford with the model E01Y and WOT2; Guy with the 15 cwt Ant and perhaps even the 4x4 Quad-Ant; and Morris-Commercial who produced the C4/AC, the CS8, the C8/GB and others.

During the War, inevitably, some MWs fell into enemy hands where they proved very popular. After the War they remained in great demand as Government surplus, being used 'as they were' or converted, by various firms, for other uses. Notable amongst these was the Arlington conversion to forward control as a delivery van, much used by the co-operative movement.

Many MWs have survived into preservation, mainly of the GS and wireless varieties although water tankers are also to be seen. MWs are a sensible choice for many owners as they take up little space, are not difficult to work on and seem to change hands at reasonable prices.

BEDFORD'S Ubiquitous 3-tonner

Last month it was the 'MW', this month, in 'part 4' of the series, Robert Coates takes a detailed look at the Bedford Model OY

'Lorry, 3-ton, 4x2, Bedford Model OY' was the official description given to the immensely-popular, square-bonnetted 3-tonner of which 72,384 were built between 1939 and 1945. Using the 157in wheelbase of Bedford's long wheelbase civilian truck, the Model OL 3-tonner had much the same, general 'WD' vehicle specification as the MW, with its flat radiator grille and squared-off bonnet. Mechanical treatment was, however, slightly different.

The standard 3.5-litre Bedford WD engine was fitted, producing 72bhp at 3000rpm although this was invariably governed to 2800rpm; this gave a power-to-weight ratio of 11.2bhp/ton, laden, allowing a top speed of about 40mph. Maximum torque, of 161 lbf/ft, was developed at 1200rpm. As with the other Bedford WD types, a Solex carburettor was fitted in place of the civilian Zenith version, and 12V electrical equipment was used, rather than the 6V which was still civilian practice. A 32-gallon fuel tank gave an average operating radius of about 280 miles. Most military Bedfords, the OY included, were fitted with mechanical air pumps for tyre inflation with an air-line hose supplied in the tool-kit: the pump power take-off was mounted on the near-side of the gearbox, driven by the lay-shaft.

Some 300-odd contracts were placed for, or in connection with, Bedford's OX and OY models: the numbers of OYs produced are shown in the table.

In the 1944 'Vehicle consolidated key list' there are no less than 69 catalogue entries for the OY, covering the following applications:

- bread carrying
- canteen
- disinfector
- film processing
- fuel and water tanks (ex-Ministry of Home Security)
- general service truck
- horse ambulance (de-luxe, two-horse)
- office
- petrol tank, 800gal
- slave battery vehicle
- water tank, 350 and 500gal
- workshop
- X-ray vehicle

The OYD GS general-service truck differed little from those supplied by Austin, Commer, Dennis, Leyland and Thornycroft, having a flat, wooden floor, fixed or hinged sides, and hoops or bows to support a canvas tilt cover. Contracts for GS trucks amounted to over 35,000 vehicles, one single order being placed for 10,000 trucks - at £319.50 each! Other contracts for OYDs included one for 3000 and another for 4000 - specified as 'with superstructure and tilt': 50 were bought for the Admiralty. The Wheeled Vehicle Experimental Establishment (WVEE) at

Farnborough also had some for experimental purposes. At least one GS truck was fitted out as a fire tender - probably a prototype, as most Bedford fire-tenders were on the QL chassis. There were plenty of local conversions, but many of these may date from the post-war period.

The OYC was supplied in chassis-cab form for other manufacturers to supply the body. These included 350- and 500-gallon water tanker - both fitted with two hand-operated pumps, each capable of delivering 350gal/hr; later models of the 500-gallon version were also fitted with a 1000gal/hr power-operated pump. Water tanks were produced almost exclusively by Butterfields, 615 of the 350-gallon, and 583 of the 500-gallon version being supplied: almost 2000 more were built but the details are lost. Duplicate sets of filtering equipment were stored, with the delivery hoses, in a locker at the rear of the tank, and the whole vehicle could be disguised as a GS truck by fitting a canvas tilt.

The OYC chassis was also used for the 800-gallon petrol tanker - this differed from the standard version in having an additional cross-member to support the front of the tank. As with all petrol-carrying vehicles, a fire-screen was fitted behind the cab and the exhaust was re-routed to avoid hot gases coming into contact with petrol vapour from the load. The body had two compartments and was fitted with a hand-operated pump and two 10ft delivery hoses. Camouflage was

A brace of OYs being loaded on the Mulberry Harbour at Arromanche.

OYD general service truck - or 'lorry' if you prefer English - photographed at Bletchley Park last year.

Production of Bedford Model OY: 1939-45

Year	ERD* total	Chassis numbers: start	finish	total	Engine numbers: start	finish	total
1940	15,100	21001	40033	19,033	2001	10000	8000
					50001	59679	9679
1941	15,078	40034	53889	13,856	59680	77820	18,141
1942	13,557	53890	68617	14,728	77821	92788	14,968
1943	12,516	68618	79852	11,235	92789	108146	15,357
1944	9356	79853	89162	9310	108147	120712	12,566
1945	6777	89163	93385	4223	120713	129999	9287
Total	72,384			72,385			87,998

* Engineering Records Department, Vauxhall Motors, 1949

Numbers of vehicles and engines do not tally because 15,614 'spare' engines were produced; annual figures based on chassis numbers disagree with ERD totals due to differences in timing between allocation and production.

This is the similar 30cwt OXD model with a timber general-service body.

Above: Photographed at the Yeovil Festival of Transport in 1997, another very tidy OYD general service truck.

A line of general-service trucks being loaded from railway wagons somewhere in France.

The lack of front-wheel drive meant that the 4x2 OY was more easily bogged down - although this is clearly not a hole created by the truck!

benches, grinder, and so on. There was also interior lighting, various tool boxes, an anvil and other useful odds and ends. Power for the dynamo was provided by disconnecting the prop-shaft and bolting a sprocket to the end of the Cardan shaft - not a good idea if you needed to leave in a hurry!

The remaining types of OYs appeared in relatively small numbers. A total of 320 slave battery vehicles with Spurling bodies costing £311.66 are recorded. These were very similar in nearly all respects to the OX battery slave vehicle, but the larger - 20ft 5in - body of the OY accommodated more batteries.

A single X-ray vehicle was followed by a further 94 with 'arcticized' bodies built by Austin. The X-ray body, developed from an earlier design on an Albion chassis, had two compartments: the front one contained a generator and had an entrance door on the near-side with a large flap on the off-side to allow servicing from outside. The rear compartment was entered through a rear door.

Eleven 'de-luxe' horse ambulances for carrying two horses were supplied and a quantity of OYD mobile canteens with special bodies by Edward Howard and Sons was ordered for the US Army, the original order for 15 canteens, also for the US Army/Red Cross, being cancelled and redirected for British use. Another contract called for two Elliott-bodied mobile canteens in September 1944.

In the summer of 1941, 228 'disinfectors' were supplied. A prototype film-processing vehicle was built, the chassis/cab costing £275.01: Spurlings made and fitted the body for £363.04 and film equipment costing £587.97 completed the unit. Its total cost? - £1226.04 - a colossal amount for the time. A further five were ordered 'for calibration troops, RA' but there is no indication of what this might mean. Spurlings also built 35 bread-carrying bodies and 200 mobile kitchens in March 1943. A prototype mobile office was supplied on an OY chassis, with a further 40 following in March/April 1944 - the Elliott body, including 'tentage', cost £450 on top of the basic vehicle price of £270.03.

Transferred from the Ministry of Home Security were large numbers of fuel and water lorries, some of which were fitted, in

effected as with the water-tank. Contracts were placed for a total of 4210 of these vehicles, the earliest appearing to date from 1 January 1943 (although dates on old WD documents can be very suspect). Various firms produced the tanks, including Butterfields (£225), and Aluminium Plant & Vessel (£246). The Steel Barrel Company also supplied eight tanks for use with sulphuric acid and Spurlings were also said to have 'supplied' some tanks but, as this was not their normal business, it probably means they simply fitted them.

Amongst other OY types was the mobile workshop which was, initially, modified by the RASC from GS lorries by adding a range of equipment. Later, at least 653 vehicles were supplied complete, plus a further 21 for the RAF. The equipment comprised a bench, lathe, switchboard and charging board, 7.5kW dynamo and regulator, drills, vices, quasi-arc welding plant, portable forge, air compressor,

17

Left: Awaiting collection in a side street in Luton, this line of OYs on one side of the road (with MWs parked opposite) was a typical wartime scene near the Vauxhall/Bedford factory.

Above: OYD fitted with a pillbox structure and an ex-Naval gun, almost certainly for airfield-protection duties; note the armoured cab.

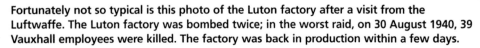

Fortunately not so typical is this photo of the Luton factory after a visit from the Luftwaffe. The Luton factory was bombed twice; in the worst raid, on 30 August 1940, 39 Vauxhall employees were killed. The factory was back in production within a few days.

available as the OYD 'Armadillo'. This was similar in most respects to the MLD 'Armadillo' but was fitted with extra skirts thus giving it only 8in ground clearance. There are records which show OYs in use as road- or, more probably, runway-sweepers but, like the fire tenders, these may date from the post-war period, being local conversions.

There were probably lots of other conversions made to this versatile and reliable 3-tonner but, when all is said and done, there's plenty to play with!

The first step on its journey to a new, restored life, this 'find' is on its way to the private collection of a life-long Bedford enthusiast in Surrey.

July 1942, with Hasler equipment on a trailer for use with smoke-screens: apparently over 1800 vehicles were supplied in this way. A producer-gas powered version of the OY GS truck was built, experimentally, which necessitated having a shorter body to accommodate the gas-producing equipment.

There were, of course, lots of modifications for special purposes, many of which are probably unrecorded, but one such, carried out by the RASC, was a modification of the GS version to a stores vehicle. This entailed fitting wire mesh covers over the normal superstructure and above the tail-board. Steel bins were located under benches, with compartments for small items of equipment above the benches. A writing desk and correspondence basket completed the picture. Another 'mod', known as the SP 3-pounder, carried out during the 1940 invasion scare, was to fit a Great War 3-pounder (1.85in calibre) Naval coastal-defence gun on the rear. This was

mounted, on its pedestal, on a drop-side OY, the sides lying horizontal to form a working platform when in use, with the tail-board hanging loose. The gun traversed 360° with geared elevation from +25° to –35°; maximum range was about 4000yds.

An armoured version of the OY was

A Naval OYD at what appears to be some sort of demonstration at a dockyard: it certainly does not have the authentic ring of a genuine 'action' shot.

WD numbers for the various types ran in the following ranges. The numbers are not necessarily continuous within the ranges and, doubtless, others were allocated outside the ranges shown.

Bread carriers	L5819791-5819825
Disinfectors	L52116-52155; L526511-526524
Film-processors	L5570918 (prototype); L5592505-5592509 (production)
Fuel and water tankers	L4684868-4685065
Fuel tankers	L167443-167500; L511636-526814; L4532267-5818747
GS lorries	L178509-240845; L510101-529606; L4144714-5869879
Horse ambulances	L516413-516423
Mobile canteens	L5154755-5154769
Mobile kitchens	L5204797 to L5204996
Mobile offices	L5469702 (prototype); L5575551-5575590 (production)
Mobile workshops	L206236-240769; L510113-579567
Slave-battery vehicles	L4661590-5306961
Water tankers	L236525-237192; L515062-521440; L48292640-5300007

BEDFORD'S MODEL OX

Last month we looked at the Bedford OY. This month Robert Coates tells us all about the Bedford OX, essentially a short-wheelbase brother to the OY, which was used as both an 'artic' and as a rigid chassis

The Bedford 'Model OX' was available in two basic forms. Firstly, a rigid-chassis vehicle which, to all intents and purposes, was a down-rated, short wheelbase OY for operation at 30cwt. And secondly, a tractor for use with a semi-trailer, suitable for payloads up to around tons. Both the rigid and the 'artic' version were derived from the short, 111-inch, wheelbase of the O-Type which, in civilian life would have been known as the OSC in chassis-cab form, or OSD in 'general-service' format, and the OSA ('A' or 'artic') respectively. Bedford's model nomenclature can be a bit of a puzzle if you don't have the key - see table.

IN common with all Bedford's wartime production, OX models were fitted with the six-cylinder 28 HP engine - often, mistakenly, referred to as the 7-horse engine which was, in fact, the pre-war offering. Power, on the 30cwt GS version was kept down to 16.45bhp/ton by governing engine revolutions to 2580rpm, whilst torque was 161 lbf/ft at 1200rpm. This meant that the 'official' top speed was 0mph, but the use of 'Mexican overdrive' (free-wheeling, out of gear) allowed speeds well in excess of this to be achieved, especially downhill, laden! Other OX rigid models had more-or-less similar power-to-weight ratios, but the power-to-weight ratio of the 6-ton 'artic' version fell to round 8 or 9bhp/ton, depending upon the governor settings. Most other aspects of the mechanical specification were very

Right: A view of the Scammell automatic coupling, as fitted to the OXC tractor unit. The idea was that the trailer could be coupled and uncoupled without the need for the driver to leave the cab. Electrical connections were made via rubbing plates on both unit and tractor. This example is actually taken from a post-war Scammell catalogue but the general arrangement is identical.

This beautifully restored OXC petrol tanker, dating from 1943, was photographed on Madeira Drive, Brighton, on the HCVS London to Brighton run in 1998. It is in the livery of the Petroleum Board and, for the year in question was, undoubtedly, the vehicle the author would most have liked to take home!

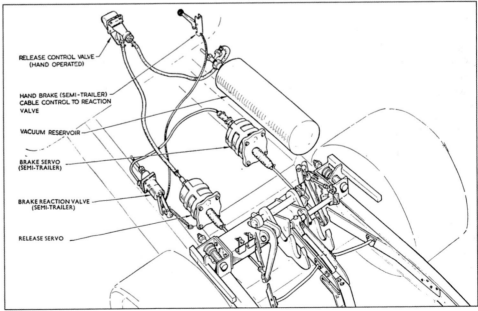

RELEASE CONTROL VALVE (HAND OPERATED)

HAND BRAKE (SEMI-TRAILER) CABLE CONTROL TO REACTION VALVE

VACUUM RESERVOIR

BRAKE SERVO (SEMI-TRAILER)

BRAKE REACTION VALVE (SEMI-TRAILER)

RELEASE SERVO

OXC with an enclosed 6-ton house-type body for use as part of a command and signals convoy.

Bedford's (peacetime) vehicle nomenclature

Bedford model designations can be a bit of a puzzle. This list attempts to sort out some of the more common reference letters.

B	special 'cargo' body with tilt and winch ('Model RL' only)
C	chassis-cab only - body supplied by other manufacturers
D	dropside truck; special 'charging' body on RL
E	platform truck
F	special 'cargo' body with tilt and winch ('Model RL' only)
H	special appliance body ('Models RL and S' only)
P	platform truck
R	fitted for wireless
T	tipper; or anti-tank tractor on MWT; troop carrier on QLT
V	van
W	fitted with winch
Z	chassis only

OYD 3-ton GS lorry carrying a Mk 2 wooden 'Armadillo box' for anti-aircraft defence of airfields.

similar to the MW. There were semi-elliptical springs and hydraulic shock absorbers on all four wheels, and a 24-gallon fuel tank which gave an operating radius of around 240 miles.

Production of the rigid version was cut back after 1940 to give greater emphasis to the OY and QL models, but the 'artic' remained in production until the end of the War.

The 'standard' OX was the OXD GS ('general service') truck in which an enclosed, steel-panelled cab provided seating for the driver and one passenger, with a flat floor and detachable cover and superstructure at the rear. This version was used for a multitude of tasks. Some were used as fire tenders for the RASC and had to be fitted with draw-bar gear to enable them to tow a pump trailer; at least one was converted to a meat carrier. 'Battery slave' vehicles were sometimes converted to 'battery charging' trucks and at least eight tippers were ordered (census numbers, L4483026-4483033). Doubtless there were many other, 'unauthorised', conversions too.

The 'rigid' OXC was generally supplied as a chassis/cab for the body to be fitted by others. However, there was a single factory-fitted variant of the OXC - a mobile canteen, mainly used by Civil Defence and fitted with a Spurling-built, 'Luton' style, body, with let-down flaps in the side from which hot food and drinks could be dispensed. Many were sign-written with the name of the sponsoring individuals or organisations. At least one book on Bedfords refers to them as an MW 'tea-van'. Although it is just possible that such a conversion was made on the MW chassis, it seems unlikely since the MW was on a shorter wheelbase and would have been far less satisfactory for the job.

'Battery slave' trucks were used mainly for starting tank engines in the field and were heavier than the GS version, grossing 9750 lb laden. The body was constructed by Spurling, and was modified from the GS version by adding higher sides to give about six feet of internal headroom.

Very-nicely restored OYD 3-ton GS general service lorry. Despite its lack of all-wheel drive, if the GMC 2½-ton 6x6 is the classic American cargo truck of WW2, this must surely be the British equivalent.

Equipment included benches on either side, with battery racks between and beneath; they were also equipped with power-take-off, servicing tools, jumper cables and a mass of electrical equipment. The battery banks were 'tapped' to give 10V, 20V or 30V output for starting vehicles equipped, respectively, with 6V, 12V or 24V electrical systems. A slightly-different version was available for battery charging.

The OXA 'anti-tank truck', or 'Armadillo', was an interesting but unattractive little vehicle, and is dealt with in more detail on page 22 of this issue. The simple armoured body had two apertures with sliding shutters fitted at the front, in either side and, at the rear, in the entrance door: the roof also had an aperture. The driving compartment was entered from the body.

Finally, we come to the OXC articulated tractor unit which was based on the peacetime Bedford-Scammell 'artic' and was designed for use with a 6-ton payload. The tractor weighed a shade over two tons, unladen, and was 189in long. Scammell automatic coupling gear was fitted, and the vehicles were mostly converted by Scammell themselves, but Taskers also carried out quite a large number, the cost of the conversion being £31.25. The OXC was used by all services - the Royal Navy

and the RAF used them for a wide variety of purposes, but in the army, they tended to be confined to rear echelon, depot, duties. There were many contracts for this version and one of the earliest for OX/OY models was for conversion of 30 OXC chassis-cabs to 'artic' tractors. In February 1941 an order for 15 Bedford-Scammells was placed 'for the RAF' and in January 1943, a batch of tractors - H4230195 upwards - were constructed and charged to Canadian Forestry. In addition to those of Scammell manufacture, trailers were provided by Brockhouse, SMT, F&S, British Trailer Company (BTC), and others.

Amongst the many applications of the 'artic' version were 'signals cabins', some

of the bodies for which were constructed by Strachans; these vehicles also had to undergo modifications to enable them to tow a wireless cabin. Street washers are also recorded but probably the bulk of OXCs were used to haul petrol or water tankers. Supplied as a complete unit, factory options included two types of three-compartment petrol tanker, both having chassis-less construction, and both made by the Steel Barrel Company. One was of 2000-gallon capacity, the other being 1200-gallons. Oddly, the water tankers were not supplied complete, but as a tractor unit only, semi-trailers being provided by a number of different suppliers, under separate contracts.

Other factory-produced combinations were the 'standard semi-trailer lorry' which had a 20x7ft load area with 3ft-high fixed wooden sides. This compares with the flat-platform lorry which had a 15x8ft deck. Both types of trailer, and the coupling gear, were supplied by Scammell.

Also intended for 'GS' cargo duties were the drop-side lorry and an extra-large flat platform version. The drop-side semi-trailer was constructed on a step-frame giving a load area of 19ft 9in x 8ft; the sides hinged down in three sections - the rear-most two sections on each side were three-feet high, whilst the smaller, front section measured only 18 inches. Tyres were 32x6, dualled at the rear. The extra-large 'high-loading' flat platform semi-trailer had a huge loading platform (33ft 2in x 7ft 2in) and ran on larger, 10.50x20, tyres. There was also a special torpedo-carrying trailer with four single 10.50x20 tyres, in line, at the extreme rear.

Possibly the most famous of all the semi-trailers was the low-loading unit, more usually known as the 'Queen Mary' which was used for recovery of damaged aircraft both our own and the Luftwaffe's. These Taskers-built semi-trailers were 34ft long by 6ft wide with 30in skeletal sides and a central superstructure designed to assist in the task of carrying aircraft components. Overall length was around 50 feet on a (combined) wheelbase of 37ft 2in, and a familiar post-war sight was the

Another very attractive OXC petrol tanker, this one in army camouflage markings.

tailboard warning notice 'caution - 50 feet long' which was, in those days, a very long vehicle and not one to be stuck behind!

Finally, there was the 'Bevin Bus', run by the Ministry of Supply Transportation Department. The body for this monster, which had a carrying capacity of 65 people, was built by C H Roe on a Dyson semi-trailer. It had a shaped front end to the trailer to minimise the gap between tractor and trailer and measured, internally, 24ft 7in. The Royal Navy used some of these, converted to mobile classrooms.

Note that the census numbers for 'artics' were prefixed 'H' to signify that trailers were exchangeable. The exception to this, for the OXC, was with the 'Queen Mary' trailer manufactured by Taskers of Andover, which was permanently coupled by means of a large ball-joint. When the trailer could not, in normal operation, be uncoupled, the census number began with an 'L'.

As with most wartime vehicles, conversions for various special purposes were carried out, a notable one being a pantechnicon used by the civil authorities.

Of all the wartime Bedfords, fewer OXs have survived than any of the other models, and there are very few surviving trailers. Possibly the reason for this is that, with the exception of some tankers and Queen Mary trailers, they were too valuable in civilian life. After de-mob, most were worked to death and subsequently scrapped.

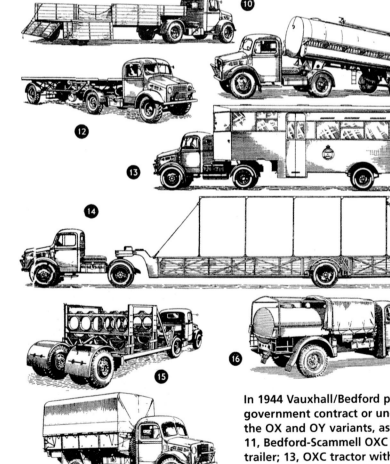

In 1944 Vauxhall/Bedford produced a handy guide to vehicles supplied under government contract or under Ministry of War Transport release. This shows some of the OX and OY variants, as follows: 10, Bedford-Scammell OXC 6-ton drop-side lorry; 11, Bedford-Scammell OXC petrol tanker; 12, Bedford-Scammell OXC 3-ton Tasker semi-trailer; 13, OXC tractor with Dyson or BTC bus trailer; 14, OXC 3-ton tractor with Tasker 'Queen Mary' semi-trailer; 15, OXC tractor with torpedo-carrying trailer; 16, OYC 3-ton petrol tanker; 17, OYD 3-ton GS lorry.

BEDFORD'S QL... part 1

This month, Robert Coates begins to look at Bedford's 3-ton 4x4 - the ubiquitous QL of WW2

BETWEEN 1930 and 1948, Bedford produced a total of 554,865 vehicles for the War Department and, during the War years alone, built an astonishing 215,258. Of these, 52,248 were QLs - just under a quarter of the total output. Their 'functional' appearance, with a flat, sloping front and high ground clearance, probably make them the man in the street's idea of a WW2 army lorry. They were also popular with the men - and women - who had to drive them and, even to those who did not, their characteristic sound - part engine and part tyre noise but, mostly, the whine from the four-wheel drive transfer case - could be very endearing. Whilst not as noisy as the Austin K5, the QL had a similarly-distinctive sound and, for many, the QL, too, earned the nom de guerre of the 'Screamer'.

The QL was produced in six principal versions:

QLB Bofors light anti-aircraft gun tractor
QLC chassis-cab only
QLD general service cargo
QLR fitted for wireless (FFW)
QLT troop carrier (sometimes known as TCV - 'troop-carrying vehicle')
QLW tipper, equipped with winch

QLD general service cargo

The QLD was the Army's most numerous off-road 3-ton general-service load carrier and was used wherever there was an off-road requirement, and later in the War became the standard three-tonner. The QLD had a metal body with a wooden floor, into which were cut trap-doors to give access to the chassis. Recesses were set into the tops of the sides to accept the tilt-bows, or hoops, over which the canvas

A very early QLD general service lorry - if not the prototype itself. Note the central strip down the radiator - abandoned very early on in production, as was the circular Bedford badge, being replaced with a small stamped metal rectangle. There is no anti-aircraft hatch and the wheel-hubs lack the later lifting-flange. The tyres on the rear wheels also indicate something out of the ordinary.

The description 'custom bodies' would have included this mobile shop built by Milburn Motors Ltd of Glasgow. It comprised the front part of a QL imposed on a Tasker 'prefab' trailer. By retaining the front wheel drive, the floor height has been kept to a minimum.

body was hung. Tilts were usually a simple rectangle of canvas lashed down along the sides, with large flaps to fold in at the front and rear: some tailored versions also appeared, especially after the War, when they had been 're-canvassed'. The tailboard, which lowered right down for loading, was provided with D-shaped foot-holes to act as steps for access.

'Air-conditioning' in the cab was effected by opening the windscreens, the machine-gun hatch, both windows and the sliding metal panel in the rear bulkhead - even then, it could still get fairly hot! If it was cold outside, a 'heater' was available by opening the inspection cover on the engine casing and allowing warm engine fumes into the cab!

A QLD in its TCV (troop-carrying) role, in Cyprus. The Army number, 33YW79, indicates that this vehicle had a simple overhaul after the War and did not require any 're-work'. The tubular 'fence' across the front of the body is an afterthought.

The first and the last QL contracts included orders for general service cargo QLDs. The first, dated 8 February 1940, covered 4272 vehicles, of which 2501 were QLDs at a unit price of £411.20. The last was dated 23 May 1945, calling for 2000 tropicalised and APT (air-portable) vehicles. This latter contract was marked 'break

Vauxhall Motors

22

Tank Museum

A QLW, winch-equipped tipper with, for whatever reason, a tilt! It seems very likely that these were used as simple load carriers when their services as a tipper were not required. The presence and absence of various features show this to be very late production as, indeed, QLWs did not come upon the scene until 'the last minute'. The census number indicates 1945 production and the vehicle shown has all the 'goodies' - flanged hubs, AA hatch, no central radiator strip, rectangular badge, but still features the long obsolete gas-plate beneath the driver's windscreen

The rations truck from B Echelon, The Wiltshire Regiment, in Krefeld, Germany in 1949. The crossed keys insignia on the front wing represent 4 Infantry Brigade.

The author's QLD GS. The flanged hubs can clearly be seen and, just, the AA hatch in the nearside roof. The starting handle is, unusually, mounted to the left - the conventional way was to the right, the position being changed on petroleum versions (ie, tankers) because there were exhaust-pipe modifications which had to be accommodated.

PRACTISCH NIEUWE

BEDFORD VRACHT- WAGENS

met vooraandrijving: 200 tot 1000 km. gelopen. Slechts voor f 2500,— per stuk af onze opslag- plaatsen. Bedrijfsklaar. Met reserveband en wiel Type QL x 4,3 ton, met stalen cabine en bak. Bandenmaat 1050 x 1100/20-. Verder alle onder- delen van bovengenoemde Bedfords.

N.V. „KRAANBULL"
Kralingseweg 291 - 293, Rotterdam.
Telefoon (010) - 130640; na 18 uur (01896) - 2142

QLs were not just offered in the home market. This 'Bedford fracht wagen' is offered 'met vooraandrijving' (right-hand drive).

clause' and was reduced to 392 vehicles, L6272781-6273172: although census numbers up to L6274780 were allocated, they were not taken up.

October 1944 saw the first contract for 4000 QLDs which were both APT and '...suitable for use in the tropics'. These were priced at £444 ex-works and were numbered L6124332-6128331. At least two of this batch are known to have survived: L6125084, released from service as 47YW62 (chassis 48097), is kept at Horley, Surrey, and L6125561, latterly 43YW60 (chassis 48998), was the author's proud possession.

QLDs were often used as the basis for experimentation - eg. for waterproofing - and they were also frequently converted to other types including tankers, fire tenders, field kitchens and the like. Many other contracts were also placed for GS cargo lorries, some having subtle peculiarities written into them for some special item or other. For example, one contract called for 252, out of a total of 2000 vehicles, to be 'converted to fuel & water' but,

unfortunately, no details of what this conversion involved have been found. Others required the fitting of mine-detector equipment in a swivel-mounted rear drum, and two were supplied to the WVEE but, again, no record of how they were used has come to light. Yet another was for a QLD to be supplied to the BBC for use in the transmission of live broadcasts from the field during and after the D-Day Normandy invasion. Other contracts for GS cargo lorries called for 'outside' suppliers to fit GS bodies on to QLC chassis/cabs.

QLT troop-carrying vehicle

With its extended chassis and body, the QLT troop-carrying vehicle (TCV), usually known as the 'Trooper', differed in appearance from the QLD. It also needed an extended exhaust pipe to cater for the longer body, to carry exhaust fumes well to the rear, away from the passengers - a feature which could usefully have been adopted on the QLD TCV: one could almost choke to death in the back of the 'D' version! Being based on the QLC chassis-cab, the Trooper had twin 16-gallon petrol tanks and the spare wheel was carried in a cradle under the rear of the chassis.

Instead of a conventional tailboard, most QLTs - those with all metal bodies built, predominantly, by Austin but also by

A QLD GS in the REME collection when it was still housed at the School of Electrical and Mechanical Engineering at Borden, Hants. The census number is bogus, possibly having been added for film work - many QLs featured in the film 'A Bridge Too Far'. This one is (or was!) in perfect mechanical condition and exhibits a post-war tailored tilt.

Marshalls of Cambridge - were fitted with rear doors. With the aid of a step attached to the rear of the chassis, this enabled passengers simultaneously to board on both the left and the right-hand side. However, bodies were also put out to other contracts, and some of these can be identified by having wooden bodies and conventional tailboards. As with everything produced within the fog of war, there are exceptions to this, but both types were fitted with access doors at the front of the body on each side, giving four formal entry and exit points.

Disembarkation - always in a hurry, of course - meant that over the sides and over the (still-closed) tailboard became informal exit points. This could indeed have been a 'giant leap for mankind' when it is realised that the deck height was around 48in, and the closed tailboard height over 72in high!

REME HISTORIC VEHICLE

23

Another view of L6215561 showing the post-war tailored tilt which, though it still 'weighed a ton' was a lot lighter than the war-time rectangular tarpaulins.

The overall length of the QLT was 21ft 10in compared with the QLD's 19ft 8in. Including the space vacated by the petrol tank and spare wheel, this allowed an additional 3ft 5in on the body length so that it could accommodate 30 troops seated, with kit, plus the driver; 29 were 'inside' and one 'up front' who took care of any action required from the AA hatch immediately above his head.

The 'trooper' was also popular for carrying loads because of the extra body space it offered. Use in load-carrying mode entailed folding back the side seats and removing the centre seat-assembly which was then stowed in a recess under the floor. Standing instructions were that the load should be carried well forward to maintain traction and steering effort on the front axle but it was pointless asking a part-load of troops to sit forward as they all wanted to see the world go by! On some vehicles, which had seen repeated boarding and disembarking of troops (or loads) across the tail, the chassis extension tended to sag a little - hence its affectionate name, the QL 'Drooper'

The first contract for QLTs, dated July 1941, calls for '1050 QLC for modification to QLT', with the chassis extension being added by Austin, who also provided the bodies. The vehicles were supplied at a chassis-cab price of £359.80 the troop-carrying body added a further £186.63. Deliveries started in August 1941, and,

being an early contract, WD numbers were allocated at the time the Army received the vehicles. So the RASC had L557230-558029 except L557654 (a total of 799 vehicles), and the RAOC had L4591022-4591271 plus L4591409, a total of 251 vehicles. One sometimes wonders just how the official mind works in allocating numbers in this way! The fate of at least one of these vehicles is known: L557599, re-numbered after the War to 61RE86, was posted to the RASC in BAOR in 1968 and was probably reworked to a GS office body.

QLW winch-equipped tipper

The QLW 'winch-tipper' did not appear until towards the end of the War when they were widely used by the Royal Engineers for clearing debris and building airfields. Because the winch was deemed to be a useful feature in this role, the prototype was constructed on a stripped-down QLB chassis and it seems likely that uncompleted QLBs and other 'unwanted' QLB production was diverted to QLWs.

The driver's controls on the QLW were different from other models, even the QLB. There were four 'gear'-levers, the two usual ones for the main and transfer gearbox controls plus, as on the QLB; the control lever for the Wild or Turner winch gear. A fourth lever controlled the hydraulics for the tipping gear. This usually had three, notched, positions: forward to raise the body, and back to lower it; the central position was for when the pump was out of use. Some versions had a different arrangement for lowering, with the 'back' lever position operating the tyre-inflation pump.

At least three contracts were placed for this model, the first being for the prototype based on the QLB chassis, followed by a batch of 946 vehicles, most of which were non-APT. Deliveries started

After the War, QLs were snapped up by civilians who needed some form of lorry transport. Some firms, such as Scottorn, specialised in refurbishing QL chassis and, when required building new 'custom' bodies.

in December 1944 with all those supplied after 23 February 1945 being to 'tropical' specification. The price was £550.04 complete with Edwards Bros (Edbro) tipping gear. One contract source includes a record of an amendment dated 11 August 1946, indicating that work may have continued on QL production after hostilities had ceased, but this is unreliable and no cross-reference has been traced. The last contract was placed very late in the War and was cancelled before any deliveries took place. It is believed that 1947 QLWs were supplied, in total, with the D and T models standing at 25,704 and 3373 respectively, but these figures may not be precisely accurate.

After the war, thousands of surviving QLDs, Ts and Ws were sold to civilians where many were worked to death. When new, they offered an amazing performance - by 1945 standards - with around 10bhp/ton, laden, plus colossal tractive effort (1490 lb/ton), so quite large numbers found work in vehicle recovery and timber extraction. Many have survived into preservation although, amongst these, there is often to be found quite a large element of re-build and cannibalisation.

The QL story will be continued next month...

Bedford's publicity photograph of an early production troop-carrying vehicle (TCV), the Model QLT. Note the under-slung fuel tanks which allow the body to extend right up to the back of the cab; the spare wheel was stowed under the tail. Also, the radiator strip is now discontinued but the AA hatch is still not 'fitted', neither are the flanged hubs. QLTs usually had a tailored tilt, as shown, as distinct from the simple rectangular tarpaulin of the QLD.

Vauxhall Motors

BEDFORD'S Fighting QL

This month Robert Coates takes a look at the aggressive variants of one of the most versatile British trucks of WW2, the 3-ton 4x4 Bedford QL

WHILST the QL was designed and developed as a logistics vehicle whose purpose was the transport of military personnel and materiel, its ruggedness and versatility soon caught the attention of the War Office. In spite of its 'B', or 'soft-skin' classification, it was destined for other, non-logistic and less passive roles - if carrying ammunition to guns in the front line can be called passive! These roles included some tasks which were downright aggressive, amongst which was that of the QLB.

The QLB towed a Bofors 40mm 'ack-ack' gun, replacing the Morris CDSW 6x4 tractor unit. It remained in service throughout the war years and was ultimately replaced by the 6x6 AEC Militant as anti-aircraft guns became heavier and more sophisticated.

There was little wasted space in the back of a QLB; it carried a crew of nine, with seating for the driver plus one crewman in the cab. The remainder sat 'in the back' with five in the crew compartment and two more between the rear lockers. There were doors on either side of the crew compartment fitted with detachable side curtains, and there was a sliding panel in the roof for ventilation. In the rear of the body there was a quantity of 40mm ammunition - four cases each side - plus other equipment required for such a role, including a spare gun barrel stored amidships, and a spare gun-wheel, stowed behind the crew compartment. The rest of the crew's personal and fighting kit was kept in a variety of containers and lockers.

Power winches were fitted to QLBs to assist with manoeuvering the trailer and for recovering itself from bogged-down positions. There were two types of winch - the Wild gear, produced by M B Wild & Company, had angled winch-sheaves and 183ft of steel wire rope; the Turner winch, from the Turner Manufacturing Company, had horizontal sheaves and 175ft of rope. In basic specification and performance they were almost identical: both had a maximum rope pull of 6 tons with the drum unwound, or 4 tons with wire wound on to the drum - the pull being less with rope wound-on because of the tendency to cut into line already on the drum. With the engine running at its maximum governed speed, rope could be wound-in at the rate of 209ft/min, so, in a hurry, both could wind-in the lot in less than a minute, unloaded.

QLBs weighed-in at about 6 tons 12cwt with all their kit aboard; to this was added the weight of the gun and trailer, which varied depending on which version of the trailer and 'mark' of the gun were attached. ▶

Pictures of the anti-tank portee seem to be in short supply. This official, record shot gives only a sketchy idea of what one looked like when ready for business - especially with the tilt rigged. The ATP's armament is of interest: known as the 6-pounder 17 cwt to distinguish it from other types of 6-pounder in use, it had a 57mm calibre and theoretical range of 5500yds although it was never used at that range. First orders were placed in June 1940 but deliveries did not start until all necessary production of 2-pounders had been completed. Later versions could pierce armour at least six inches thick at 1000yds and 30° angle of attack.

Tank Museum

IWM, E22437

The 8th Army crosses into Tunisia on the northern section of the coast road in February 1943.The stripped down appearance of this QLB has been achieved by removing the 'air-portable' cab top: it is not a 'rag-top' QLC! The Bofors gun is trailed with the gun in its usual transport position, with the barrel horizontal. Note the 51st Highland Division's addition to the Italian kilometre post.

'Watch the birdie!' Posed, slightly-ridiculously, in theoretical operating positions, this shot gives a rough idea of the Bofors 40mm light anti-aircraft gun in operation. The Bofors was of Swedish design and manufacture but after an initial purchase of 100 guns and half a million rounds of ammunition, a licence to manufacture in Britain was negotiated.

QLB disembarking from a Class 9 ferry on the 'far side' of the Rhine. This photo is slightly unusual for the period, as divisional markings, clearly visible (but unidentified) were almost invariably obliterated by the censor.

Pre-delivery, factory shots of the basic QLB. From fairly early production, it has yet to be equipped with its POL containers and spare wheel. The two long boxes on the bed of the vehicle hold 48 rounds of 40mm Bofors ammunition each side; immediately above them, in two groups of two, are the lockers for general equipment; the third locker on the second row contains, on the nearside, a tool roll, wheelbraces and oil-can and, on the offside, the snatch-block, shackles, hawsers and towing rope. The two tractor scotches can also be seen in their recesses behind the rear mudguard.

QLBs which served in the Western Desert were usually marked with an RAF roundel on the roof for identification purposes.

The first ever production contract placed for QLs of any type called for 1771 QLB Bofors LAA together with 2501 QLD general-service lorries: clearly, their suitability had become apparent during the initial acceptance trials. These went into service identified, incorrectly as it happens, L4483034-4484804. The 'L' prefixes here are incorrect because the QLB was a gun

tractor and should thus have had an 'H' prefix.

One other contract is also of interest. The last of a batch numbered - this time, correctly - H5366221-5367453, was sent to the Wheeled Vehicle Experimental Establishment (WVEE) at Farnborough where it became the prototype QLW - the winch-equipped tipper - entering service as L5367453.

By 1945, contracts had been placed for about 5500 QLBs, representing more than

10% of all QL production and many were, after their wartime use, converted to GS cargo bodies.

Other fighting QLs included the 6-pounder anti-tank gun portee, more accurately referred to as a 'portee and fire' vehicle. This was developed to improve the mobility and flexibility of anti-tank weapons in the war in the desert. Built on the QLC chassis, it is quite often referred to - even in official records - as a QLB, from which it differs in almost every important respect, making it unlikely that QLB chassis were ever used.

The idea of carrying the gun, rather than towing it, was not a new development and, in fact, was first tried out during the Great War. One of the problems with a towed gun was its general vulnerability and lack of manoeuvrability, whereas a

Factory shot of the QLB complete with all the canvas covers to the rear part of the body; note the shadow camouflage pattern.

gun which could be mounted on the vehicle could, in today's terminology, 'shoot and scoot'. The 6-pounder field gun which formed the armament for the outfit, could be towed, but was much more usually carried, and there were three different ways to do this.

In fighting trim, the gun could be mounted so as to fire forwards over the canvas-topped cab. To achieve this, various preparations had to be made. Importantly, the radiator had to be protected and a large anti-blast plate was provided for the purpose; at the same time, the cab top, sides and windscreen were folded down, and the gun-trail had to be split.

The gun could also be mounted to fire-off rearwards which, again, entailed having the gun-trail split but, in this configuration, the cab top and sides could be left intact. The vehicle could be driven with the gun in either of the fighting positions but, for really going places, the 'touring trim' was used, with the gun out of action, facing forward over the cab and with the gun-trail unsplit.

The 6-pounder was loaded and off-loaded using two hand-winches, the gun-wheel and central trail ramps for which were carried in a locker beneath the body floor. They were needed when changing position from forward to rearward firing-off - thankfully a task which did not have to be performed all that often. At the rear, a steel superstructure supported a detachable canvas tilt inside which were four, demountable, tip-up crew seats. There were 96 rounds of ammunition carried in lockers, and gun shields were fitted to the sides of the body.

The anti-tank portee had, as fitted on all QLC chassis, standard, twin 16-gallon tanks mounted underneath the body thus giving the maximum deck-length and putting them well away from the flash of firing guns! Of passing interest is the arrangement of these two 16-gallon tanks. Fuel was first drawn from the right-hand (off-side) tank. When this ran dry, a tap brought the nearside tank into use, this one having a four-gallon reserve which, itself, was accessed by turning a tap. It was very important to remember to return all taps to the start position when refuelling otherwise disasters - like running dry at a crucial time - could occur.

It seems that the first batch of portees was made up from a contract originally intended for '1126 QLC lorries 3 ton 4x4 (T)' - ie, for conversion to 'troopers' which was changed to the anti-tank specification, (on which the 6-pounder gun cost £90.59). The second, and last, contract, for 2406 anti-tank portees, was slashed to 388 vehicles and the specification was changed to GS cargo bodies - but of a special kind. Built by Brush Coachworks, these had wooden bodies and open cabs, for use in the desert, and were delivered between December 1942 and June 1943.

Similar bodies were fitted to Austin K5 and CMP 3-tonners and, after the War,

The QLB chassis - itself a derivative of the QLD, with winch gear fitted - was the basis for the QLW which came into service much later in the War. This one was, in fact, originally destined to be a QLB (H 5877076) but was used as the prototype QLW. This chassis is fitted with Turner winch gear, identifiable by its horizontal sheaves.

many of the survivors of these types were converted to GS cargo bodies, retaining their 'rag-top' cabs.

Amongst the more unpleasant roles for which QLs were used was that of the mobile flame-thrower, or 'Cockatrice'. Although more commonly associated with tanks, mobile flame-throwers were actually developed on lorries, with the intention of using them for home defence. There were two rival designs in the early stages of development - one from Lagonda, the other from AEC. Lagonda's effort was built for the Petroleum Warfare Department, and used a sort-of armoured van on a Commer chassis. The AEC contender, known as the 'heavy pump unit', was far more substantial. The design work is attributed to J C Rackham, a tank designer and Tank Corps officer who had worked for AEC before the War.

The outcome of this experimental work was two production versions of the Cockatrice. The heavy Cockatrice, of which six examples were built and allocated to the defence of RAF stations, was based on the diesel-engined, 6x6 AEC Model O856 which was rather like a six-wheeled Matador. The regular Cockatrice was similar in its general design but was smaller, being based on the QL chassis. For some unknown reason, only 60 out of the 69 ordered went into service, to be used

around the country mainly for the protection of Royal Naval Air Stations.

Specified as being 'fitted for carriage of FUL equipment', bodywork for the Cockatrice was supplied by Ratford Metal Bodies and the price for the vehicle, body and all its equipment was £405.94. There appear to be no records of their performance in service - if, indeed, they were ever used - but, as one authority remarked, 'whilst they may not have been beautiful to look at, they looked stark and aggressive enough - and apparently worked quite well, at least on trial'.

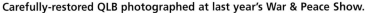

Carefully-restored QLB photographed at last year's War & Peace Show.

BEDFORD'S QLC 'ARTIC'

In the eighth part of this series, Robert Coates describes the now very-rare Bedford QLC - a 5-ton 4x4-2 tractor/semi-trailer combination

ALONGSIDE all the factory-built QL variants, QLC tractors were supplied in chassis/cab form for bodies to be fitted by manufacturers other than Bedford. They were almost identical to QLDs except that they had twin petrol tanks under the body and the spare wheel was stowed at the rear, the QLD having both behind the cab. Altogether, about one in seven QLs produced were QLCs, representing a total build of just under 7000.

The QLC was used for many and varied applications including development and experimental work. It was the basis of the 'Trooper', the 6-pounder anti-tank portee, the Cockatrice and the articulated tractor/trailer combination.

As such it was designated 4x4-2, the military way of saying that a four-wheel-drive vehicle had a two-wheeled trailer. Its load was carried in what, today, appears somewhat unusual, with 1 ton in a small drop-sided body on the tractor and 5 tons in the trailer. There were two reasons

Vauxhall drawing of the QLC, clearly derived from the one of the QLC photographs included here - even down to the disposition of the shadows.

for this odd-looking arrangement (which was sometimes known as a 'dromedary' - or two-humped camel). Firstly, for load distribution reasons, the turntable coupling had to be placed directly above the rear axle and on the standard QL 143in wheelbase this left a huge space between the back of the cab and the front of the semi-trailer which not only looked wrong, but wasted an awful lot of vehicle. To fill the gap, a 'dog-box' was fitted. Secondly, with a substantial load resting over the rear axle, traction on the front axle was reduced so a ton added at the for'ard end helped to keep the front wheels on the ground.

Although modifications to the standard chassis were

relatively few, three are worth highlighting. First was the need to cut off the rear ends of the frame side-members - they served no useful purpose on the articulated version and the steel could be used elsewhere at the same time as saving weight on the tractor unit: also additional cross-members had to be fitted to carry the trailer coupling. Secondly, the brakes had to be modified to cope with 6-ton, rather than 3-ton, loads. Gross laden weight increased to 24,416 lb, compared with the standard QL's all-up weight of around 16,800 lb. The brake modification required a vacuum reservoir tank and its accompanying vacuum gauge in the cab for the driver. Finally, and also to cope with the additional weight, the rear shock-absorbers were uprated.

The technical specification of the QLC tractor, apart from the differences mentioned, was the same as for other military Bedfords except, of course, that it had very different dimensions. The length of the tractor and semi-trailer together was 30ft 6in; it was 7ft 6in wide and 10ft 8in high: the semi-trailer alone was 17ft 8in long.

Two manufacturers, Glover, Webb & Liversedge and the Scottish Motor Traction Company (SMT), were involved in building the trailers, which were all built to the same design - basically a 'general service' body with a flat floor - unlike the QLD GS truck which had wheelboxes - and a detachable canvas tilt and tubular steel bows.

The trailer was permanently coupled to the tractor by a 6-8 ton ball coupling which was manufactured by Taskers of Andover. The coupling allowed up to 20° of tilt either side and fore-and-aft which, it was felt, made reasonable allowance for rough ground or for climbing or descending small hillocks. The brakes on the trailer were operated, whilst on the move, in the conventional way, being linked into the vacuum-servo assisted footbrake system - hence the need for an additional vacuum reservoir. An additional brake, in the form of a lever fitted to the trailer, was supplied to hold the vehicle when parked. It could

only be applied from ground level and it was rather important to remember to release it before attempting to drive away. At its full gross weight and with the trailer handbrake on, 72bhp was simply not enough! Single rear tyres were retained, both on the tractor and the trailer, to improve cross-country performance - a slightly academic feature on the trailer as the wheels were not driven and any deviation from straight ahead would, because of 'tracking', have nullified the advantage. It was, however, cheaper than twin rear wheels and much easier to maintain. A spare wheel for the trailer was carried in a retractable carriage above the trailer axle.

The recommended 'trailed weight' for the 4x4-2 on normal roads, was 6 tons, double the load rating for the standard QL. For hilly roads it was recommended that this was reduced to 4 tons and, for cross-country work, to 3 tons - giving little or no advantage over the 3-ton capacity of the rigid QLD. At 6-tons load - representing nearly 11 tons all-up - progress must have

A QLC 4x4-2 articulated combination, dating from 1942, clearly showing how it obtained its nickname 'the 'dromedary' or two-humped camel. One ton was carried in the 'dog-box' on the tractor unit with a further 5 tons - in on-road conditions - in the semi-trailer. These 4x4-2s carried an 'L' prefix to their census number since, in the normal run of events, the trailer was not detachable, but note how the census number (on all the QLCs shown) is spaced into two groups of figures with a dot separator.

Tank Museum

been rather leisurely, even on normal roads, as the engine was the same as in the rest of the Bedford range - including the MW 'pneumonia- wagons', which were only rated for 15cwt. That the same engine could be used across such a wide weight range was, of course, all due to gearing and whilst, to gearbox technologists, it may not seem surprising that there was only about 16% difference in gear ratios across the whole range of vehicle weights, the fact that there was an 800% difference in weight between the lightest and the heaviest Bedfords does strike one as slightly amazing.

The first record of QLC 4x4-2s appears on a contract dated 25 April 1942 (number V4810) which called for 1080 and production started soon after. The batch was allocated numbers running from L558030-559109, with the prototype being L555423. Most artic tractors are capable of being matched to different trailers; in other words, they are interchangeable. In such cases the unit was considered simply as a tractor and was given an 'H' prefix to its census number. If the trailer was not detachable, as was the case with the QLC tractor, the tractor unit and its trailer together were allocated an 'L' prefix - although interestingly this theory does not apply to the WW2 Scammell Pioneer tank transporters which were numbered 'H' even though the trailer was similarly non-detachable. In fact, of course, in both cases the trailer was detachable, but this was a workshop job requiring special equipment and, in normal day-to-day operation, tractor and trailer remained firmly attached.

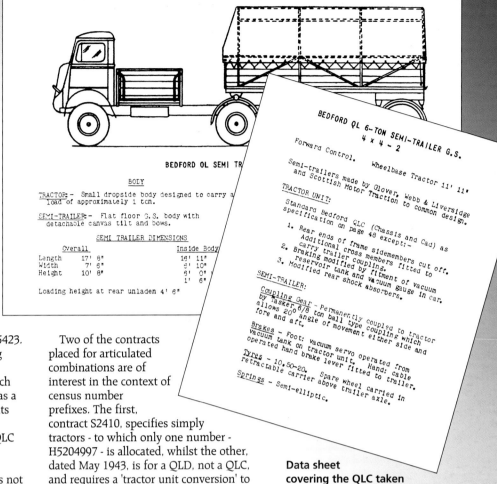

BEDFORD OL SEMI TR[...]

BODY

TRACTOR:- Small dropside body designed to carry a [...] load of approximately 1 ton.

SEMI-TRAILER:- Flat floor G.S. body with detachable canvas tilt and bows.

SEMI TRAILER DIMENSIONS

	Overall	Inside Body
Length	17' 8"	16' 11"
Width	7' 6"	8' 10"
Height	10' 8"	6' 0"
		1' 6"

Loading height at rear unladen 4' 6"

BEDFORD QL 6-TON SEMI-TRAILER G.S.
4 x 4 - 2

Forward Control.   Wheelbase Tractor 11' 11"

Semi-trailers made by Glover, Webb & Liversidge and Scottish Motor Traction to common design.

TRACTOR UNIT:

Standard Bedford QLC (Chassis and Cab) as specification on page 48 except:-

1. Rear ends of frame sidemembers cut off. Additional cross members fitted to carry trailer coupling.
2. Braking modified by fitment of vacuum reservoir tank and vacuum gauge in cab.
3. Modified rear shock absorbers.

SEMI-TRAILER:

Coupling Gear - Permanently coupled to tractor by Tasker 6/8 ton ball type coupling which allows 20° angle of movement either side and fore and aft.

Brakes - Foot: vacuum servo operated from vacuum tank on tractor unit. Hand: cable operated hand brake lever fitted to trailer.

Tyres - 10.50-20. Spare wheel carried in retractable carrier above trailer axle.

Springs - Semi-elliptic.

Data sheet covering the QLC taken from the War Office handbook of standard vehicles; note how far the semi-trailer is from the cab despite the presence of the 1-ton 'dog box'.

Two of the contracts placed for articulated combinations are of interest in the context of census number prefixes. The first, contract S2410, specifies simply tractors - to which only one number - H5204997 - is allocated, whilst the other, dated May 1943, is for a QLD, not a QLC, and requires a 'tractor unit conversion' to be carried out, suggesting that it, too, was a prototype, but for a different specification. Weight is added to this conjecture by the 'H' prefix. It seems likely, therefore, that these two contracts were both for prototype artic tractors with a detachable trailer, one on a QLC chassis and one on a QLD, both probably fitted with the Scammell automatic coupling gear. Retention of the 143in wheelbase, together with the unusually-high ground clearance of the QL, would have rendered a solution involving a detachable trailer impossible at economic cost.

The QLC artic combination tended to be confined to depot and rear echelon work and was thus something of an anachronism with its four-wheel drive. If a fully-detachable artic combination was required there was always the very versatile Bedford-Scammell OXC to do the job.

During 1943, QLC artics were shipped to North Africa where they serviced the docks at Phillipville taking stores and supplies inland to Constantine. This is a very hilly area and the trucks worked hard and long - to the extent that two weaknesses became apparent: Firstly, constant use on wide throttle openings, laden and uphill in low gears, caused the exhaust valves to burn out - which would probably have been the case with the OXC as well. Secondly, the trailers had a habit of overturning - which might not have happened with the lower profile of the OXC.

A remedy for the burnt-out exhaust

valves was soon found - by using valves from tank engines - Churchill tanks had engines designed and built by Bedford, in the form of an opposed flat '12'. This, apparently unlikely, cure is reported to have worked!

The second problem was harder to solve. The trailer was permanently attached to the unit by a very simple ball-joint. The lugs which carried the retaining bolts for this coupling suffered metal fatigue and often broke, resulting in the trailer overturning. This seems hardly surprising given that the allowable play on the coupling was only 20° in any direction - quite satisfactory for road conditions but on the 'thin' side for rough ground. It is, of course, not known whether the lugs broke causing the trailer to overturn, or vice versa for QLs were notoriously easy to overturn with over-exuberant application of steering lock.

So hard-worked were these vehicles in North Africa that many finished up as scrap at the Return Vehicle Depot at Bizerta; some were loaded into landing craft, taken out to sea and dumped; others were taken over by the Italians when the British returned to the UK.

Not one seems to have survived into preservation.

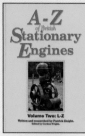

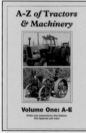

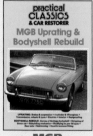

Bedford QL
tankers and fire tenders

Robert Coates continues the story of Bedford's 4x4 QL of WW2

APART from the articulated combination or 'dromedary' which was dealt with in last month's issue, Bedford's QLC chassis-cab was put to many uses. Amongst these were troop-carriers, mobile kitchens and canteens and, possibly most numerous of all, tankers.

These QLD Fire Tenders were from the initial batch of 299 vehicles supplied against contracts placed in June 1943. The bodies were built by the Austin Motor Company and 14 of them were specially prepared for use in the arctic! The tilt-bows are of non-standard design (for QLs) to accept the extension ladder which was suspended from them.

Tank Museum

Seen languishing in an 'off-limits' area at the Imperial War Museum at Duxford in 1993, this Brockhouse tank-trailer is waiting for someone to apply a little TLC to bring it back to being a very scarce and worthwhile exhibit.

Large numbers of tankers were used by the armed forces for petrol, aviation spirit, lubricants and water. Most of them were supplied on 4x2 chassis which, from Bedford, centred on the MW, OX and OY models, although some were supplied (or converted) from the pre-war civilian-type Bedford OL 3-4 tonners with twin rear wheels. Those supplied on QL chassis, whilst basically similar, were of many different specifications.

Major users were the RAF, who had several basic types of fuel tanker, early versions being of 1000-gallon capacity. These came complete with 'pto' (power take-off) for driving on-board pumps. The power take-off, a feature of several different QL roles, including the QLB, QLR and the winch-tipper QLW, was taken from a point on the transfer case and was operated by a remote engine-throttle control.

By the end of the War, contracts had been placed with Butterfields of Shipley, Yorkshire, for 950-gallon tanks to be supplied, this type also being supplied to the Army. The 950-gallon version had two rear and two side lockers. The rear lockers housed a total of eight lengths of hose; six for fuel delivery - 123in long and 1.5in bore - and two for suction - 134in long and 2in bore. In the nearside compartment was a small petrol engine - either a 3bhp Bradford or a P5XC Stuart-Turner - which drove, via worm reduction gears, two drum pumps, usually manufactured by the Slough-based Zwicky company, for fuel delivery. The side compartments also carried an air-separator, pumping control valves, two flow-meters and a suction filter.

Fuel delivery capacity was 30-40 gallons/min through one boom and nozzle, or 55-65 gallons/min through two.

It was a requirement for fuel tankers that the chassis had to be fitted with a full-depth guard behind the cab to ensure that no sparks or 'stray heat' came into contact with fuel vapours. This meant that the window shutter in the rear of the cab had to be blanked off, and the exhaust system also had to be re-routed, with its outlet just beneath the radiator. This re-routing of the exhaust pipe required some of the frontal appendages on the cab to be fitted the reverse way round, particularly noticeable being the starting handle which was mounted to the left instead of the right. Some tankers, such as the Bedford OYC, were fitted with attachments to accept tilt-bows - with a tilt over the top of the tank, there was nothing to suggest to aerial reconnaissance that the vehicle was a tanker, and thus a prime target. This idea does not seem to have been used on QLs.

A variation on the standard fuel tanker was the RAF's aircraft-refuelling tanker. These were fitted with either two or three booms mounted on a platform at the front end of the carrier tank, for over-wing filling. Each boom had 12 feet of hose and terminated in a trigger-type filling nozzle. The outer two booms were connected to the fuel system and the centre one to the oil system, the booms themselves being 13-feet long and described as 'self-elevating'. This is something of an understatement as the

springs which 'assisted' the self-elevation were extremely powerful and quite capable of lifting a man from the ground unless carefully controlled, as discovered by the author when working on 19AD40 in 1985 - the year in which the vehicle was found, in a barn - still carrying 40-year old springs!

The three-boom version had a two-compartment tank, divided to hold, at the front end, 100 gallons of lubricating oil and, in the rear compartment, 850 gallons of fuel. After the war, when the vehicle was in use for refuelling, or defuelling, turbo-prop aircraft with AVTUR (AViation TURbine fuel) - the lube-oil compartment and its associated boom was not used.

On occasions, tankers were used with a trailer. These were usually manufactured by Brockhouse and, when towed behind QLs, used the standard towing hitch on its leaf-sprung coupling. These Brockhouse-produced trailers were examples of what was known as the Bellamy type, having a four-wheeled chassis and a tank of 900 gallons capacity. They had a triangular, 'A' frame drawbar and a swivelling towing-eye and were usually equipped with a Lister 42QA petrol engine driving Zwicky pumps. Another, different, specification of Brockhouse trailer was also available - the Brockhouse Mk 2 - which had a capacity of 5 tons, but there is no evidence of these having been towed by QLs.

Fuel consumption of the standard rig was estimated at 7mpg - compared with 8mpg for the standard cargo versions - or 5mpg for 'camp-running' which, inevitably, involved mostly low-gear work and, on some versions, use of the power take-off.

Tankers on airfield duties logged very low mileages (19AD40, the airfield refueller referred to earlier, had 1200 miles on the clock in 1985 and was in a condition which suggested that this was a genuine reading!) As a result, some of them were very long-lived and many were re-worked just after the War and in the early 'fifties, again, mainly for the

Rear view of the QLD 1000-gallon water tanker showing the petrol-engined pumping gear.

Tank Museum

RAF. Many tankers which survived the services had a second lease of life as civilian bowsers of one sort or another and several have survived into preservation. At least one ended up in Australia where it was found derelict a few years ago, this fact having come to light as the author received an enquiry as to exactly how the exhaust pipe should be routed! It appears that the wreck had been used as an irrigation bowser, had 'conked out' somewhere in the outback and had simply been abandoned. How it came to be there in the first place remains a mystery.

Although built on the QLD chassis, it seems perfectly appropriate to deal with fire tenders at this point. Fire tenders were supplied mainly for guarding airfields and for the protection of fuel and ammunition dumps and, as such, had two distinct functions - the rendering of first aid for smaller fires and, for more extensive conflagrations, serious fire-fighting.

The basic body of the vehicle was externally similar to the metal-bodied GS lorry with tilt, except that it was 6in longer at 242in overall. Four lockers were cut into the front part of the body, and there was a shallow tail-gate flap, to permit rapid access. Its main equipment consisted of a 200-gallon water tank mounted centrally in the forward end of the body together with a first-aid hose reel mounted between the

body and the cab; there was also a pump which was driven from the pto and, as with the tankers, hand-controlled by a remote engine throttle. This equipment, which fulfilled the first-aid role of the outfit, could be put into action instantly on arrival at a fire.

For fires which required rather more than first aid, a trailer pump was towed, usually with either a Coventry Climax or a Godiva pump. Fixtures were provided on the vehicle to carry a hook ladder as well as a 30-foot extension ladder which was hung from the tilt superstructure and which protruded both fore and aft. Side-lockers were fitted in which to carry the suction hose and all the necessary nozzles for the trailer pump, together with various types of fire extinguisher. For shipping purposes the trailer could be stowed in the body of the vehicle.

Finally, to make it quite distinctive, it carried a warning bell - compulsory equipment for all fire-fighting equipment! - and a large red board proclaiming 'Army Fire Service' across the top of the windscreen. A giveaway for identifying fire tenders which may, later, have been converted to other

roles, is the rear wheel-arch which is cut out in 'three-penny bit' style, rather than having the rectangular shape of the conventional wheel-arch.

The prototype fire tender was ordered on a contract dated April 1943 and was delivered in June, census number L5204998. The chassis/cab cost a touch over £347 and the body which, on this prototype, was built by Brush Engineering, cost £535. Several other contracts followed, the first being later in June 1943, for another 299 complete vehicles (L5294819-5295117), the building of the special fire-tender bodies being sub-contracted out to the Austin Motor Company. By November 1943, a further contract had been placed for yet another 150 vehicles (L5458288-5458437) so, clearly, the specification was fulfilling the requirements set for it. Finally, in July 1944, a contract was placed for no less than 553 chassis of which 290 (L5863231-5863520) had bodies built by Eccles; the remainder (L5863521-5863783), which were to have been built by Austin, were cancelled.

With an all-up weight of just under 6.75 tons, the fire tender was a little livelier than some of its more heavily burdened brethren so, after the War, they were in strong demand, some finding their way into 'private' use as fire tenders for industrial premises. Few seem to have been preserved. GYR 706, belonging to John Harrison, of Blackpool, was seen at the Honiton Hill Rally in 1998, reportedly ex-Pioneer Corps, it was painted red after a spell of 'civil' service and, at the time, was largely unrestored. Another sighting, some years ago, was in the yard of L W Vass at Ampthill, Bedfordshire - this one was also painted red and had the wrong tyres fitted but was otherwise in very tidy 'nick'.

Do readers know of any others that have survived?

This RAF water tanker is of the earlier, 1000-gallon pattern although it features the diagonal straps which were fitted to later models to strengthen the front mudwings which eventually tended to sag as the wing provided the final step on the climb into the very high cab. For some reason, the chassis of this vehicle has been 'adorned' with a very civilian-style legend, 'not to exceed 20 mph' and details of its laden and unladen weights. *Tank Museum*

Bedford QLR

Robert Coates continues his series on Bedford military vehicles by examining the house-bodied QLR

So easily confused with a QLR this is, in fact, a QLD 'mobile operations room type J145', built for the RAF but diverted to 'other duties' in 1944. It does not take much imagination to realise that the 'other duties' were in connection with the Allied invasion of France and the ensuing battle for Europe.

THE QLR was the house-type model used for all command and communications, and most office applications. There were three basic versions - original, command (HP and LP types, wireless), and a 'new' TEV type.

And that's where it stops being simple!

The original version was available with any one of eight different body types: 'cypher'; 'command' (HP and LP); mobile terminal carrier; two 'terminal equipment vehicles' (TEV) at Divisional and Corps level; and three wireless bodies - 'wireless (1)', 'wireless (R)' and 'wireless HP'.

The 'command' and 'wireless HP' models were eventually superseded by the second version, supplied with an improved L-shaped tent which could be erected along the nearside and rear of the vehicle.

The original TEV was superseded by the 'new' TEV, which could be either type A, B or C; the 'type C' was the heaviest, at 6 ton 15cwt gross. These new TEV types had a 16ft body and were mounted on a chassis similar to that of the QLT. A later - post-war - type known as 'TEV Div' or, occasionally, as 'body 15 (unfitted)', was similar to 'body 2 (unfitted)' which was, basically, the 'command' version body. Many of these, some of which were post-war rebuilds, soldiered on, often with very low mileages, into the 'seventies, which is why so many

office-bodied QLs have survived. Many of these rebuilds are, for convenience, known as QLRs, since they are similar in appearance to the 'real' QLR, even to the extent of having been fitted with generators and radio-suppression equipment. However, to the purist, they remain converted QLTs!

Mechanically, the QLR was much the same as other models but had fairly sophisticated radio-suppression equipment on the ignition, distributor and spark plugs. They were also fitted with a power take-off, from the rear of the transfer gearbox, to the special 660W auxiliary dynamo.

Equipment varied between roles, but was very comprehensive. For example, in the wireless role, the internal, or 'staff', section of the body was fitted with a full-width, double-sided map-board and a full-width desk for three men. Seating consisted of a revolving seat with a folding stand for the commander and, for the other staff, there were two sliding seats ▶

Awaiting their turn for rescue, restoration and 'tender, loving care' these two were found 'off-limits' at the rear of the Tank Museum at Bovington, Dorset. It is difficult to be 100% certain when identifying QLRs, especially from photographs, but it seems likely that the vehicle photographed from the front was originally a 'terminal equipment vehicle' which has seen some post-war re-work. The second vehicle, photographed from behind, is believed to be an LCV or 'line of communication vehicle'. The louvred panels on the offside quarter are for ventilation of the generator compartment.

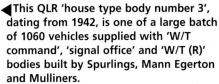

◀This QLR 'house type body number 3', dating from 1942, is one of a large batch of 1060 vehicles supplied with 'W/T command', 'signal office' and 'W/T (R)' bodies built by Spurlings, Mann Egerton and Mulliners.

£401.25 included bodies built by Mann Egerton, and were required at the rate of 60-70 per month, starting in February 1943. Orders for bodies were also placed with Spurlings, who built 200 'cmnd wireless' bodies, and Mulliners, who supplied the remainder as 'house type A GS wireless HP53 unfitted'.

In addition to the Army types available, the RAF had several designs of their own. The basic RAF 'signals' body was the 'type J' - a sub-set of the 'original' version but often fitted on a QLD type chassis: these were available in three sub-types - 102, 103 and 106. The other main RAF type was the 'mobile operations room', which incorporated wooden-framed double-skinned insulated walls. On this version, the gap between the cab and the body was often filled by a compartment erected above the spare wheel and some versions even had a 'Luton' extension above the cab.

The first contract for QLRs for the RAF called for a single QLC chassis-cab 'for mounting of prototype signals body (QLR)'. The body for this was built by Mulliners, as a 'signals type 145'. Other sources refer to it as a type 102 or 103, 'similar to RAF signals types supplied by Dennis Bros'. The contract was placed on 9 July 1943, calling for delivery in August and that neither Bedford nor Mulliners wasted any time is indicated by its being into the paint-shops on 4 August! The chassis-cab cost £353 and the body (listed as a 'Dennis signals body') cost £357, giving a total cost for this prototype of £710. This was followed by production orders on a number of contracts. One called for 23 vehicles to be supplied to the RAE with J type 145 'mobile ops room' bodies built by Dennis Bros (L5455220-54555242). These, too, were needed in a hurry and, to achieve the required date, Bedford were instructed to deliver 'at the expense of other contracts'.

Other RAF - and Army - types existed, some of which embodied 'local' interpretation of design and specification. Some were not even QLRs, but house-bodied QLCs - just to add to the general confusion! The body types which were available up to 1945 were often confused,

with lockers, plus a further folding seat. Also in this compartment, on the offside door, was a hinged table, and there was a sliding glass window in the partition.

In the 'operations' section of the body there was another full-width operator's desk plus two operators' seats, each with stowage underneath, and a central operator's seat with a drawer underneath it. To keep things cosy, the auxiliary engine compartment and the wireless set were also in this part of the body. Externally, the fittings included a sliding glass window in the roof, a luggage grid, two folding tables, a locker housing the tent, the vehicle's exhaust cowling, an auxiliary exhaust silencer, a roof ladder, cowlings for the 12V extractor fans, a louvred grille for the fan in the wireless set, stowage for engine ramps and aerial masts, a full-width kit locker and further locker units to house three cable drums and eight batteries, non-skid chains, and a 20-gallon drinking-water container! There was also a rectifier box, fuel for the auxiliary engine, a jerrycan, a fourth cable drum, and an oil can.

◀The 'house body TEV (terminal equipment vehicle) number 15' for the QLR was a later version of the 'number 3 body', there having been, it seems, no intermediate numbers! The vehicle in the photo is both APT (air-portable) and 'tropicalised' and dates from 1944.

Many firms were engaged in the production of bodies for the QLR, amongst them, Brush Coachworks, Carbodies, Car Cruiser Caravans, Dennis Brothers, Elliott, Mann Egerton, Mulliners, Normand, Park Royal, Spurlings and Strachans. Dennis Brothers manufactured horseboxes and similar equipment in peacetime, and should not be confused with the Guildford-based company, famous for fire engines and, later, municipal vehicles, who were engaged on other war work. Mulliners built large numbers of office and house-type box bodies for QLs and, in some cases the WD contract was placed direct with them, often simply for 'QLR bodies'- type unspecified.

The QLR body was prototyped by Car Cruiser Caravans. Allocated WD number L5509984, this was the most expensive QLR ever built. The chassis/cab cost a fairly standard £429.45, but the prototype body cost £765.55, making a total vehicle price of £1195! Following successful prototyping, a whole batch of production contracts was placed with Bedford on 17 October 1942.

Two of these contracts, calling for a total of 900 vehicles at a chassis-cab price of

Many office bodies could be extended, by means of tents, to give additional - and cooler - accommodation. This is one of a batch of 180 built by Elliotts and, again, illustrates how difficult QLR identification can be. This is, in fact a QLC office body - the early deliveries against the contract being non-APT, but those after chassis number 47038 had the full APT treatment, a feature which was rarely brought into operation.

37

Most of this batch of 26 QLRs went to the RAF as type J145 'mobile ops rooms' built by Dennis Brothers and were delivered very urgently, 'at the expense of other contracts'. This one, though, ended up with an S106 body, complete with its modest Luton extension, and dates from 1944.

One of the 'new' type QLRs with a TEV-type body fitted on to an extended chassis - ie, like that of a QLT. This one has the HT TEV type B body, built by Mulliners. Post-war, many surviving QLTs were also converted to this role. The contract against which this was supplied also required 'type 15' bodies and even some 13ft 'shell container' lorries.

even in official circles, because the differences between them could be quite subtle. As an example: bodies called for on one contract, dated June 1942, are variously referred to as 'studio W/T' (wireless telegraphy), 'house type number 1' and 'wireless LCV' ('line of communication vehicle'). References to this order appear in other sources and amongst the divers descriptions applied are QLR W/B 143 (variously interpreted as meaning 'wireless body type 143' and as 'wheelbase 143 inch' - which is, of course, the wheelbase of the QL). Other descriptions include 'HP type K, c/w/wireless' and 'cypher office - medium - unfitted'. Other documents refer to 'type K', 'type 10 cypher office', 'type 8 R & I', 'type 9 TEV Div & Corps', 'command HP' and 'W/T body 8 U/F R & I'.

No wonder there was confusion!

Some of this mixed batch (L4919331-4919580) saw service with 21st Army Group, which became BAOR, in north-west Europe in 1945. One was supplied to the RAOC, possibly for experimental purposes.

Finally, three contracts are of special interest. The first, placed in February 1944, called for 651 QLRs of which 12 were to be fitted with special armoured bodies for RA staff vehicles (L6171625-6171636). Little information about them seems to be available, although some rather indistinct photographs are known to exist. One wonders how the QL chassis - basically a 3-tonner - coped with the weight of armour and the vehicle equipment!

Second is a contract for a fairly-late modification built on the QLT chassis, although as already discussed, these were not strictly QLRs even though their appearance was broadly similar to the 'new' TEV type. They were designated 'WD caravan for senior officers' and provided, for wartime conditions, extraordinarily-good accommodation. A fixed roof and sides were added to the QLT chassis, and the interior was divided into two sections - one for sleeping and living, the other for working. Facilities were also provided for the officer to work in the open air if he preferred, for which a side and rear tent were supplied; the tailboard folded down to make a working platform in this mode. Within the living quarters were a bed, measuring 34x73in, together with a wash-basin and dressing table, an assortment of

cupboards, and a mirror. The living area was curtained-off from the working area which contained a desk on the left-hand side, with a softwood map-board on the opposite wall. The caravan was well stocked with equipment, too, having a 30-gallon drinking-water tank, with a hand-operated pump, and 110V lighting backed-up by battery emergency lights. Numbers allocated were L5585864-5585903.

Finally the last QLR contract of all, for 240 vehicles (L6238913-6239152) to be delivered from August 1945 onwards, was cancelled. It had, though, a note pinned to it - 'one on charge awaiting confirmation' - dated 4 January 1946. Confirmation of what... and does this indicate that work was done on QLs after the end of the war?

Dozens of QLRs and supposed, or 'faux', QLRs are in preservation. Apart from anything else they convert to a very useful camper-van for rallying. If you are more of a purist and don't like to see them used thus, you are more likely to be concerned as to whether a given vehicle really is a QLR. The only sure way is to have a look underneath, to see if you can find a winch, or, if you are clever enough, to determine whether QLR suppression equipment has been fitted to the ignition and distributor or, finally, find the factory identification plate - it should have the letters 'QLR' before the chassis number!

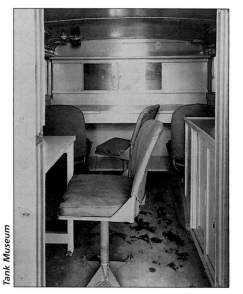

A group of LCVs 'keeping out of harm's ▶ way' in February 1945. Each vehicle was in constant communication with one of the major cities in the UK, thus providing a channel of two-way communication.

◀ An interior shot of a QLR 'wireless type K' showing just how cramped conditions were in these office-type bodies. Remember, too, that there were batteries, a petrol engine driving a generator and precious little ventilation, and some idea of the prevailing conditions can be imagined.

Robert Coates rounds off his look at the Bedford QL by describing some of the more unusual variants

SOMEWHERE, locked away in the archives of what is now the Ministry of Defence, there must be a little booklet entitled '101 useful things to do and make with a Bedford QL'. Few chassis can ever have been adorned with such a rich admixture of miscellaneous types than the QL. Standard offerings included a general service cargo lorry (QLD), troop carrier (QLT), radio/signals 'van' (QLR), gun tractor (QLB), chassis-cab (QLC) and, towards the end of the War, a winch-equipped tipper (QLW).

By the end of the War, almost every one of these had derivations: general service lorries were available in at least two versions, one having a 'rag-top' cab, having

been converted from a desert gun portee. An additional troop carrier was available, derived from the QLD; QLTs had been converted to radio shacks and, to be forever confused with specially-equipped radio-vehicles, office bodies appeared on QLC and QLD chassis. And as for the chassis-cab itself, this was used for a wide miscellany of types, although not a single one is listed in the 'Data book of wheeled vehicles - army transport, 1939-1945'. However, research in museum archives and elsewhere has turned up a wealth of less-common types.

Most numerous are probably the house-type, or box, bodies. These were fitted mainly on QLC chassis and included the 'studio W/T' and the 'TEV corps type C', both being very similar to bodies on QLR chassis. Also included are mobile kitchens,

◄ **One of the many container-style bodies adopted by the RAF. This one is a generator lorry which was sometimes used as an alternative to a towed trailer. The QLD general service body has been replaced by a flat floor on which is mounted a plinth to take the generator.**

Interior of a mobile kitchen.

of which many hundreds were built. The first reference to them is hidden amongst an order for QLDs which was 'interfered with' by extracting one of them (L4912911) to be prototyped as a 'field, or mobile, kitchen'. Car Cruiser Caravans made the conversion and later picked up significant numbers of orders for the production version at a price of just over £92 each, which suggests that not a lot of work was involved. Thomas Harrington & Co also supplied 'kitchen' bodies and, in their contract, much was made of the type of bins to be provided, the choice being either 'four bins S-type, four bins Y-type' at £22 per set or 'two bins S-type, two bins Z-type' at £11 per set, 'six bins Y-type, two bins Z-type' (unpriced!) or simply two bins 'S-type'. Frustratingly, no information can be found as to what all this means.

Very similar to the mobile kitchen in general appearance, was the mobile canteen, the nearside of which was fitted with a serving hatch. The earliest reference to these appears in 1943 when L5303128, a Type J145 'house' type, is recorded. The water is further muddied, though, as one may have ended up as a dental laboratory. The bodies were, in the main, provided by Alexanders, Scottish Motor Traction (SMT), and Spurlings.

Dental laboratories, or 'prophylactics' as clinics were sometimes called, were operated by the Royal Army Dental Corps (RADC) and were equipped with all of the paraphernalia required to operate in the field. This included the inevitable dentist's chair, medication and instrument lockers, and large water tanks. The interior, which

◄ **There is, outwardly, little to distinguish this mobile kitchen from a standard QLD with a very crude, panelled body. The inside of the body was fitted with various bins and other equipment to enable it to carry out its field function of providing a hot meal for the troops.**

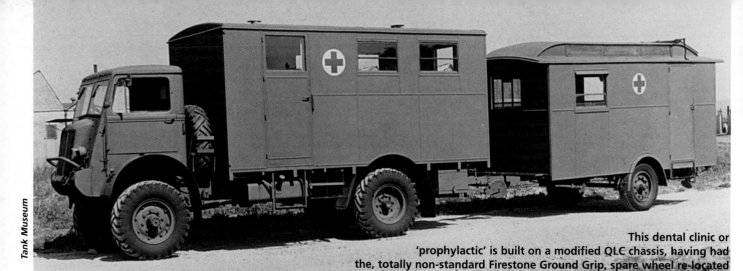

Tank Museum

This dental clinic or 'prophylactic' is built on a modified QLC chassis, having had the, totally non-standard Firestone Ground Grip, spare wheel re-located to its QLD position. Prophylactics did not normally tow trailers and this may have been a multi-purpose clinic catering for other-than-oral problems.

was painted a pale eau-de-nil colour, was lit by electric roof lamps, with natural lighting provided by three windows, high up in each side of the vehicle. Entry - and escape - was through a narrow door at the rear.

One example of the many house-type or container-style bodies which were used by the RAF, was the accumulator-charging workshop, also known as a 'battery-charging container'. There were many variants, all basically similar, but with subtle differences depending on their exact role. The body was fitted with a welded-steel frame with hardboard panelling and a sheet metal floor; sliding windows, complete with blackout shutters, were cut into the sides and in the front and rear bulkheads. Access was from the rear, by steps which could be stowed in the body. There were three battery-charging units on each side, with slotted boards on which to stand accumulators, and cupboards underneath. Against the front bulkhead were two Type 7C rectifying units and a battery-capacity testing set, together with Winchester flasks for distilled water, and a carrier for the containers of acid. Externally, along each side, a 10-foot slotted iron platform gave additional standing space for accumulators on charge. The whole unit could be serviced by an independent 230V external power supply - occasionally an enclosed trailer carrying a mobile generator set.

Surviving documents show several other house type bodies - even on QLD chassis - but the clerical records are often inconsistent and unreliable.

Various - very - special types were also built on the QL chassis and probably few more special than the 'Giraffe'. As early as 1942, detailed plans were being made for a sea-borne invasion of the continental mainland and it was realised that vehicles would need waterproofing vehicles to facilitate rapid unloading by simply driving them off beached landing craft. Experiments were carried out by several manufacturers into ways of allowing vehicles to wade without drowning the electrical system or 'inhaling' water into the carburettor. Bedford's approach was to place all of the mechanical parts which could be affected by water, effectively out of reach. The result was a strange-looking vehicle with its engine and cab raised about four feet on struts - access to the cab must have been difficult since even the standard version is quite a climb. Drive

Tank Museum

▲ Adapted from a Type J145 house body, this mobile canteen has had a large serving hatch cut into the nearside. This body-type widely used, especially by the RAF, for mobile offices and operations rooms. As can be seen, the interior is fairly spartan, before its equipment was fitted.

▶ Waterproofing was rigorously tested before being let loose, for real, on D-Day. This photograph, of a Bedford OY 3-tonner in the form of a mobile X-ray unit, is believed to have been taken near Luton or Dunstable but the precise location is unknown. The rear doors have been left open, after protecting the equipment, to prevent sinking.

Tank Museum

▶ The 'Giraffe' was one of those ideas which didn't make it into production which is, perhaps, just as well as it would have made a superbly conspicuous target.

from the engine and gearbox was taken via a chain to the transfer box mounted in its usual position. Once ashore, these towering vehicles would have made an easy target.

Fortunately, methods of waterproofing were developed using plastic compounds, which rendered the 'Giraffe' redundant.

Another one which 'didn't make it' into production was the 'Bedford Bren'. With the threatened drying-up of supplies of rubber after the capture of Singapore, and in a general attempt to save raw materials, the Ministry of Supply carried out an experiment in which a Bren-gun carrier's running-gear was mated to a standard QL. Surviving photographs indicate that, as with the 'Giraffe', a QLD chassis was used but it was, nevertheless, most certainly a 'special type'. The track and suspension assembly from the carrier was modified, mainly by shortening it, and exhaustive tests were carried out at the WVEE. This hybrid QL performed even better than had been hoped, and certainly better than existing half-tracks because, unlike the earlier marques, the QL had a driven front axle. Several reasons combined to prevent the design going into full production - its initial cost was obviously higher than two simple wheels; it was far more complex than a wheeled axle and, of course, huge strides had been made in developing synthetic substitutes for rubber which, effectively, overtook the reason for developing the idea in the first place. The prototype was either reconverted to a standard lorry or scrapped as there is no evidence that it survived or was ever used.

One idea which did make it was the 'observation tower'. During 1944, a need was identified for mobile observation towers and, needless to say, the choice of chassis was the QL. These were officially described as being 'designed to be extremely mobile, quick to operate and (give) a point of view approximately 85ft

above ground level'. Constructed on the QLD chassis 'for mobility', it could be raised, hydraulically, to full height in two minutes; lowering took less than one minute and, if necessary, the vehicle could move during this operation. The tower consisted of three sets of telescopic tubes which formed a triangular section for rigidity. It was carried, 'folded', horizontally and hinged near its centre of gravity to a frame with quick-action screws for levelling - for which a pendulum sight was provided. It was claimed that the complete levelling operation took 'only a few seconds'.

It appears that at least 10 of these towers were produced on QLs and the Canadians fitted some on Diamond Ts. Coincidentally, whilst researching these towers, the author was asked to help identify just such equipment which had turned up in Dorset

Waterproofed QLs wading ashore from a 'landing ship, tank' (LST) - as distinct from a 'landing craft, tank' (LCT). LSTs came into play after the first assault waves and had vastly superior capacity to the little assault craft.

Another idea which never went into production was this half-track known as the 'Bedford Bren'. It consisted of a slightly modified QLD mated to the running gear of a Bren carrier.

fitted on a Bedford RL chassis. It is not known whether any saw active service.

Other 'specials' included two prototypes officially known as 'tractor, 4x4-2, FBE, Bedford/Tasker' and 'tractor 4x4-2, pontoon, Bedford/Tasker' or, more simply as 'folding boat equipment and experimental pontoons' which were developed by the Directorate of Royal Engineer Equipment as articulated types. Whilst every source investigated mentions both of these, there seem to be no details surviving, and little can be gleaned from photographs. The 'FBE' was H5469698 and the 'pontoon', H5469699; the semi-trailers must have been detachable, unlike the QLC 4x4-2 which was not. The contract was placed with Bedford on 29 March 1943, calling for delivery 'not later than the first week in April' so, clearly, these had to be abstracted from the routine production on some other contract.

The price for the 'FBE' and the 'pontoon' was £344.39 each for the chassis/cab - Tasker charged a mere £24.51 for their part of the work. One can only surmise that the experiments were not successful, at least with the QL, as nothing seems to have gone into production, although there are records which suggest that more success was achieved on Albion and Leyland 3-tonners with 6x4 configurations.

Another curiosity, about which little is known, is the single QLD (L5306777) assigned to the Experimental Tunnelling Establishment which amongst its other duties researched better ways of digging trenches. As has so often been the case throughout history, generals and politicians are always preparing to fight the 'previous' war so envisaged a large role for trenches and thus a need for mechanical equipment for digging them. Delivered in September 1943, the only information traceable about this vehicle is that it was on smaller wheels and different tyres from the standard QLD - 10.50x16 instead of the usual 10.50x20 - and that its price, ex works, was £421.23.

Wartime
Bedfords for civilian use

Robert Coates takes a look at the OWS and OWL models

This 'Petroleum Board' tanker was constructed on the OWLC long-wheelbase chassis.

Nick Baldwin Collection

ALL Bedford's production during the early War years was restricted to military use but, in September 1941, two special truck models, the OWS and the OWL, were released for civilian use. Both were 5-tonners, but they were restricted to operators who were engaged on 'essential' work and could obtain a licence from the Ministry of War Transport (MoWT). Later, in 1942, a slightly-crude looking bus, the OWB, also joined the line-up.

Apart from their appearance, these models were more-or-less identical to those announced before the War started. They had the same engine, with a Solex carburettor, Dewandre-Lockheed vacuum-servo hydraulic brakes with independent front and rear circuits, and progressive suspension. They did, however, have the benefit of 12V electrical systems. The difference in appearance was confined to the bonnet, which was of the same square-nosed pattern as was, by that time, commonly-seen on the military types. Indeed, after the War, when many surplus military vehicles had been sold into civilian use, the OWL was very difficult to tell apart from the military OYD. More often than not, the OWL had twin tyres, but some did not, and just to make things worse, some early OYs are reputed to have been fitted with twin rears!

The fact that lorries were now being made available for non-military use was a huge breakthrough for those trying to

Photographed at the Abbey Hill, Yeovil rally in 1999, this nicely-restored OWSC sports the remains of a rather fancy breakdown body.

Tank Museum

The 32-seat OB bus featured the more attractive rounded nose and was generally bodied by Duple.

support the war effort at home, with increasingly aged and decrepit vehicles. Advertising copy of 1941 makes much of this - 'Here is a new Bedford for the Home Front' proclaimed one, 'and founded on the experience gained in building nearly 300,000 commercial vehicles'. The adverts made it clear that a MoWT licence was required and advised early application - 'remember it's a Bedford... and that means a waiting list for those that delay'.

These 'square-nosed' utility OWS and OWL models were discontinued in 1945, when the standard 'civvy' specification bonnets re-appeared. The OWB, which had retained its bonnet throughout, was also discontinued, and production of the pre-war truck and bus model range then continued until March 1953, by which time they were all replaced by the new 'A' types. By the time of their

Short-wheelbase OWST factory-bodied tipper.

replacement, some 412,000 K, M and O models had been built.

The engine and main chassis specifications for the OW lorries was as for the OY model - apart from the dimensions of the OWS. In turn, these were very

Long-wheelbase OWL factory-bodied drop-side truck.

similar to the OL announced in 1938 but, as already indicated, the OWs, like the OY, were fitted with 12V electrical equipment, whilst the OL still used a 6V system. This situation continued until 1950 when the OL was also fitted with 12V equipment.

Statistics for OW production (see table) show only totals, not broken down between individual models and, with Vauxhall's Engineering Records Department (ERD) figures differing from those which are generally accepted as being 'official', some detective work is necessary to obtain any useful information. However, it is believed that the figures in the table are reasonably reliable.

OWL 5-tonner

Bedford's major civilian focus in this period was on the OWL, a long-wheelbase 5-ton 4x2 truck. This shared a 157in wheelbase with the OY and was almost indistinguishable from the OYD. There were, however, some subtle differences. The OWs were fitted with a single 16-gallon petrol tank, which included a three-gallon reserve, whilst the OY had twin 16-gallon tanks, with a four-gallon reserve in the left-hand tank only.

Front and rear track on the OW lorries was 64in, the OY being 1½in narrower at the rear. The OW's turning circle was tighter, too, at 51ft 6in for the OWL, and 39ft for the OWS, compared with 66ft for the OY.

Production of Bedford model OW: 1941-45

Year	Chassis numbers:			Engine numbers:		
	start	finish	total	start	finish	total
1941	1001	5384	4384	2001	2670	670
1942	5385	12112	6728	2671	10626	7956
1943	12113	18312	6200	10627	15739	5113
1944	18313	24704	6392	15740	21470	5731
1945	24705	33591	8887	21471	31296	9826
Total			32,591			29,296

The table shows the chassis and engine numbers which appear in 'official' papers. The ERD figures differ by no more than 10% for 1942-44, but by much greater margins in 1941 and 1945. It is not at all clear why, especially as the total production figure for the period 1941-45 is the same in both cases. It seems quite likely that the disparity arises from differences in calculating the year-end, or recording dates.

There were two factory-made models in the OWL range - the OWLE flat platform lorry, and the OWLD drop-side truck. The latter was priced at £448 and was supplied in primer only, but its availability was limited by the small numbers being produced. The drop-side body was 148in long and 78in wide, with 18in sides, giving an unladen weight of 6104 lb. An additional model, known as the OWLC, was available as a chassis-cab only, priced at £405, for fitting whatever body could be obtained in wartime Britain.

Nicely-liveried OWLC in the service of Shell Petroleum in the post-war years.

OWS 5-tonner

The other major offering was the OWS, delivery of which was stated as being 'reasonably prompt'. The factory options were the short-wheelbase tipper model, the OWST which, aside from having the same 111in wheelbase as the OX, was identical to the OWL. It was fitted with a 4yd³ hardwood tipper body with a steel floor - the body was 97⅓in long and 78in wide, and was fitted with 25in sides. The tipping gear, which was of the self-priming hydraulic type, was supplied by Weston, and gave a 45-50° tipping angle.

As always, a 'C' version was available, the OWSC, for fitting custom bodywork, and this was almost invariably confined to the addition of gear suitable for use with an articulated trailer.

OWB bus

Available from 1942 onwards, the OWB was a 32-seat coach of around 6720 lb weight, on a 168in wheelbase. The body was made by the London firm Duple, and was a utilitarian version of the pre-war OB, having the 'new' rounded - 'bull nose' as Bedford preferred to call it - radiator shell,

with its external radiator filler cap. As with the lorries, the coach had servo-assisted Lockheed brakes.

Surviving military records show that 25 were ordered for the US Medical Corps in February 1945, numbered M6260664 onwards, and that these were fitted with heavy-duty tyres, 8.25x20 on the rear, and

7.50x20 on the front. Another 75, with Mulliner bodies, were ordered in July 1945.

After the War, Bedford returned to normal production, with K, M and O types accounting for over 80% of their total output from 1946 to 1948; the bulk of the remainder was accounted for by the model JC van.

Bedford's instruction book for the OWL, OWS and OWB - this example is dated 1943.

A couple of long-wheelbase OWLE flat platform trucks mixed in with some pure civilian OLB models.

Robert Coates looks at the origins of the very-successful post-war three-ton 4x4 Bedford RL

The birth of the RL

AT the end of WW2, Bedford resumed production of the K, M and O models they had announced in 1938, averaging around 30,000 units in each of the years 1946-48 - a figure which many present-day truck producers would regard with awe and envy! These models continued until they were replaced, in 1953, by the 'A Type', of which very few were supplied to the military who had, in any case, plenty of vehicles left over from the War.

In the meantime, in 1950, following four years of intensive development, Bedford announced their new 30mph seven-tonner, known as the 'S Type'. This so-called 'Big Bedford', which was the company's first civilian, forward-control offering started coming into service in 1951, and was available in four standard sizes - a rigid chassis with a 116in or 156in wheelbase, an 86in artic tractor, and a 204in, 33-seater passenger chassis.

The bulbous bull-nose and high profile made it easy to see why Bedford had chosen to call it the 'Big Bedford', and although throughout its production life, various subtle alterations were made, none was so extensive as to change its basic looks. There were differences in headlamp positioning, but probably the most noticeable was the change in the Bedford badge. Early models had, all in one, the Griffin and a small chrome strip inscribed 'Bedford', usually painted red. Later models had a separate Griffin, with 'Bedford' in individual chrome letters across the upper part of the radiator grille.

A number of factory-fitted options were available on the rigid chassis: the

An early 'S Type' short-wheelbase tipper - model SST. This 'Big Bedford', introduced in 1950, gave a major lift in payload - to 10 tons as an artic - and in cab design.

long-wheelbase version was offered as a chassis only (model SLZ), chassis-cab (SLC), drop-side lorry (SLD), and platform truck (SLP), whilst on the short wheelbase, there was a chassis only (SSZ), chassis-cab (SSC), and end-tipper (SST). The artic was known as SA, the coach chassis, SB.

The power unit was a totally-new petrol engine for Bedford, developing 110bhp from 300in³ (4900cc), and with many improvements over their long-lived 28hp offering. In fairness to Vauxhall, they had wanted to upgrade the 28hp engine from quite early in the War, but had been prevented from so doing by the War Office requirement for standardisation. In common with Bedford

practice, the new engine was a 'long-stroke' unit (4¼in stroke, 3⅞in bore, giving a slow revving and 'torquey' engine, which minimised the use of intermediate gears. The high torque - 234 lbf/ft developed at 1200rpm - made it possible to govern the engine at 3000rpm, so it was always working well within its capacity, with plenty of power reserve, helping to ensure a long life.

Listed amongst the highlights of the 'long-life' specification were slip-fit cylinder liners, chrome-plated top piston rings, Durachrome exhaust-valve inserts, a seven-bearing crankshaft, induction-hardened crankshaft journals with copper-lead main and big-end bearings, positive crankcase ventilation, full-depth

Note the subtle difference in frontal design of these later model 'S Types' photographed in 1958. These two, together with the two Leyland Beavers, were employed on long-distance delivery of non-ferrous metals from ICI Metals at Birmingham.

water jackets with directed cooling, and an extra-large, detachable oil filter unit.

A Perkins diesel option was made available in 1953, with the first 'in-house' diesel not appearing until January 1958.

Access for routine servicing was straightforward, requiring, at worst, the removal of quickly-detachable panels but, more usually, the lifting of a hinged trap. For more extensive work, such as major overhauls - don't forget that, when this vehicle was new, de-cokes were entirely common-place - the engine could be removed from the frame without dismantling the cab. The front bumper, grille and radiator were relatively-easily detached for access to the water pump, fan and associated assemblies, whilst the

front chassis cross-member itself was bolted, allowing the engine and gearbox to be extracted as one unit. Vauxhall even supplied a special trolley, fitted with hydraulic jacks, for withdrawing the engine. This represented a colossal improvement over the QL, which required the cab to be removed altogether to do any worthwhile jobs on the engine. However, in its defence, the QL went from concept to prototype in a matter of a few, war-torn, weeks, whilst the 'S Type' had taken four years of thorough, peace-time testing!

The gearbox was a four-speed, heavy-duty synchromesh unit. It was probably a delight to use when new, although Bedford's claim for 'split-second changes, up or down, on hills or in traffic', might have been a little exaggerated, as the lever travel was relatively vast, especially

between the first and second. With a few years in the log-book, and a few miles on the clock, changing gear became reminiscent of stirring a particularly-loose blancmange with a long-handled spoon. On one occasion, having carefully selected neutral, this particular driver removed his foot from the clutch, prior to switching off, only to feel the vehicle give a little jump forward - just to point out that the neutral he had selected, wasn't! Once on the move, though, and with a little practice, the 'box was a delight to use.

By the standards of the time, and from the driver's point of view, the cab was fairly-luxurious with good all-round vision. There was a fine view of the road ahead through the wide, sloping, 'V' windscreen, which was hinged at the top, allowing it to open almost horizontally. However, as the vehicle aged, and the seat springing and upholstery sagged, there was a distinct impression of sinking slowly in the west behind the dashboard, which cut off some of the short-range view of the road. Comparison with the QL, on this feature, favours the older vehicle in which the driver, perched on a canvas cushion hardly thicker than a Ryvita, and rather less comfortable, had a totally-commanding view of the road. Wide windows in the door provided good side vision and, at the back of the cab, curved rear quarter lights and a large rear glass centre panel, facilitated reversing unless, of course, you happened to have a van body!

Controls were utterly conventional. In the left-hand dashboard bezel, there was a speedo, incorporating an odometer, but with no trip, whilst the right-hand bezel, contained a fuel gauge and temperature gauge. Between the two was a Bakelite switch for the lights, the dip-switch button being operated by the left foot. The steering wheel was 'specially designed' to allow a good view of the instruments, having two spokes more or less horizontal and slightly below centre, but with an additional, ugly and apparently-superfluous vertical, plain metal spoke. The cab was reasonably well provided with storage spaces - a glove-box cubby hole with a hinged flap at the left-hand end of the dash, and lockers in each seat for tools.

The 'S Type' had an interesting braking feature, which may well have been available on other makes at the time, but if so the writer is unaware of it. The front brakes were hydraulically operated - those at the rear were mechanical, but

Seen at rallies. A nicely-restored standard box-van 'S Type' on the HCVS London-to-Brighton run and an equally tidy GS cargo RL seen at Duxford in 2001.

were actuated by hydraulics. The clever feature was in the master cylinder, which was so designed that, should a leak occur in the front hydraulic system, the pressure behind the piston would collapse and the piston would travel on until it made physical contact with the piston which controlled the rear, mechanical linkage. Thus, even with no front brakes, some braking remained available at the rear.

Some 'S Types' were supplied to the armed forces, notably the Royal Navy who used them for a variety of purposes in keeping with their policy of buying 'off-the-shelf' where a 'ruggedised' spec was seen as unnecessary. Some SB passenger chassis were supplied also, probably to all three of the services. These were adorned with various bodies, built both at home and abroad. Many were built by Strachans and had a square-ish, functional appearance which whilst not exactly attractive, was copied by other coach-builders.

Special versions of the 'S Type' supplied to the military included the SAG artic tractor unit for use with a 5-ton 'Queen Mary' trailer, and the SLG which carried a Simon platform for such jobs as aircraft servicing.

In 1953, a four-wheel drive version of

the 'S Type' was announced, to be known as the RL and, for the unwary spotter, there seem to be few differences between the two models. The trick is, usually, simply to look at the wheels on the rear axle - the 4x4 RLs have single rears and the 'S Types' have twin rears. There were exceptions to this, so it is not 100% reliable but, if you don't have time to see whether there's a diff on the front axle, this is a pretty good guide. For the real buff, it is possible to form a pretty accurate idea of the year of manufacture, as well, from subtle changes in frontal aspect, grille, lights and so on - but more of this later.

Initially, the RL was made available commercially to such customers as electricity boards and other 'civvy' outfits that needed four-wheel drive. It was not

until 1953 that the Army really sat up and took notice, rating it as a three-tonner, thus indicating it was a direct replacement for the QL. Even though the Army likes to have a bit in hand, in terms of power and payload, this did not last long and the RL was fairly swiftly uprated to a four-tonner.

There was a great variety of military RLs, ranging from the GS cargo truck through tippers, Simon platforms, fire-trucks, refuellers, tractor units, and so on. Possibly the most famous of the lot was the so-called Green Goddess which, strictly speaking, is not a military vehicle as it was supplied to the Home Office for Civil Defence use. But more of these anon.

Next month we will look at the RLs used by the armed forces.

A tantalising glimpse of some of the 1000-odd Green Goddesses kept in store in tip-top condition awaiting any eventuality. More of this at some future date.

By 1970, some of the Army's RLs had come up for disposal. This early model has been reconditioned by L W Vass of Ampthill, Bedfordshire, who fitted the wooden drop-side body and HIAB 172 lorry loader.

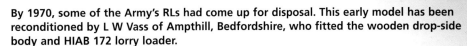

Bedford RL

Robert Coates looks at the ubiquitous RL - the military equivalent of the 'Big Bedford'

FV13184 Royal Air Force 950-gallon refuelling tanker built on the 4x2 S Type chassis but incorporating FV-pattern headlamps.

BEDFORD'S RL was the four-wheel drive version of their very successful, civilian 'Big Bedford' - the 30mph seven-tonner introduced in 1950/51. By 1953, the Army had sat up and taken notice but, as always, wanting more power in hand, the civilian seven-tonner became a military three-tonner. It was not until 1968 that it was realised that there was indeed, plenty in hand, and the payload was uprated to four tonnes.

Note the move to metric! Although many dimensions in the automotive industry were by then quoted in metric units, Bedford held fast to measuring engine sizes in cubic inches - the American way. However, other details were strictly metric - length was 6.36m; height to top of cab, 2.602m or, with tilt, 3.11m; width, 2.39m. The load area measured 4.267x2.178m, but its weight was stated either as 8800kg loaded, or

18,000 lbs maximum design weight - the two figures do not reconcile!

With the incredible precision only possible from a theorist - as distinct from a practical operator - the 'unprepared fording depth' was given as 'up to two feet, but not exceeding two feet six inches'. How one was supposed to make this very fine distinction before entering a deep puddle, beggars description. Preparation for fording depths greater than 30in consisted of covering the axle breathing vents with two layers of adhesive tape!

Other 'vital' statistics included an operating range, on roads, of 400km, and with a fuel tank of 118 litres, this represented a fuel consumption - in understandable units - of about 9-10mpg. As for its top speed, different sources quote different figures - and, in practice all of them are likely to be figments of the imagination - what an army driver can squeeze out of a vehicle often defies belief. One source states the maximum road speed as 75kph (about 47mph): the Army's Handbook - possibly a more reliable source - states 54mph in rear-wheel drive, or 28mph in four-wheel drive.

On some versions, a lever on the steering column applied the trailer brakes independently of the vehicle's brakes. It was operated by slowly turning the lever clockwise and, in conjunction with slipping the clutch, could be abused for

Photographed in November 1974, this shows the FV13142 Midge drone launch platform with the pilotless reconnaissance drone aircraft ready to go.

hill starts rather than using the handbrake. Care had to be taken to release it in good time as it usually took a little time for the brakes to 'free'. However, enough of these bad habits!

As with the S Type, changes in appearance were made throughout its production life, most of them common with the S Type. Unique to the RL, was the lowering of the headlights by some seven inches because the four-wheel drive and strengthened suspension raised their height above that allowed under the civilian 'Road vehicle lighting regulations'. Special drawings were issued by Bedford for the conversion which was carried out at dealerships.

The cab of the RL would be readily recognisable by drivers of the civilian Big Bedford although there were, of course, little odds and ends which 'militarised' it. The addition of a (brass-cased) carbon-tetrachloride fire extinguisher was one. This is frequently missing from vehicles in preservation as they are quite hard to come by and a collectors' piece in their own right. In service, it was not unusual to find that they were either empty or somewhat depleted - carbon tetrachloride is an excellent, if rather dangerous, dry-cleaning agent and was marvellous for removing greasy stains from uniforms!

Mechanically, the RL was almost identical with its civilian brother, although the track was greater to accommodate larger tyres without increasing the turning circle. The (petrol) engine was of particular significance and interest, being an all-new Bedford product of 300in³ (4.9 litres), developing 130bhp gross, or 98bhp at the clutch - compared with the 78bhp of its 3.5 litre predecessor. At sea-level, and at a maximum gross weight of 18,000 lb (a shade over eight tons), the power-to-weight ratio was a respectable 11.7bhp/ton. Apart from size and power, the 4.9 litre engine had many technical refinements and was more sophisticated than its predecessors. It also had a different sound compared to the old 28HP unit which it superseded.

The sound of an old Bedford is quite unmistakable - and very endearing to those who count themselves amongst the vast band of Bedford enthusiasts.

Bedford had produced their half-millionth vehicle in 1947, being the first British manufacturer to achieve that total, so they were a familiar sight - and sound - on the roads - 'You see them everywhere' the slogan said, and, of course, you heard them everywhere, too. With fairly modest upgrades since 1931, including the uprating from 27 to 28HP, the same engine design had been used throughout and none of the alterations seemed to have affected its unique sound. Whilst the new engine had a different sound it was, nevertheless, quite definitely a Bedford!

Reverting to technical matters - the

The classic GS cargo-bodied RL with the later-type grille, lowered headlamps, military-type sidelamps and indicators, and a full set of canvas on the steel body.

Vauxhall Motors

gearbox was a synchromesh four-speed unit. There was also a transfer box which, as on the QL, engaged four-wheel drive at the same time as engaging low ratio: the lever for this was on the extreme left, with the gearlever to its right. The 4-ton winch - where fitted - was run from the power take-off (with first gear engaged) and was controlled by the central lever.

Sometime about March 1962 - from chassis R34137 onwards - a revised specification for the electrics was introduced, consisting of a new, six-position lighting switch, combined stop-tail lights, two stop-light switches, sidelights and 'turnlight' (ie, direction indicator) equipment.

The RL was available from the factory in a number of different formats and, to some extent, the variety of body types was similar to those provided during WW2 - general cargo, workshop, signals vehicle, tanker, and so on. Bedford, as

Early RL photographed on the FVRDE test slopes during the 1956 exhibition of British military vehicles at the Chertsey site - note the unmodified headlamps and civilian-type sidelamps.

usual, had their own nomenclature for these, as follows:

- RLB - special cargo body, with tilt
- RLC - chassis-cab, non winch equipped
- RLD - special charging body
- RLF (and RLW) - winch-equipped chassis
- RLH - special appliance chassis (eg, for 'Green Goddess')

However, things had become more sophisticated since 1945 and 'FV' numbers were assigned to various ranges

Sample FV13100 variants

FV13101	GS cargo
FV13102	Container, stores, binned
FV13103	Charging - signals
FV13104	Power generating and charging - MT batteries
FV13105	Cargo, with winch
FV13106	Fuel tanker, 800gal
FV13107	Mobile electronic laboratory
FV13108	Photographic laboratory
FV13109	GS cargo, FV body
FV13110	Signals
FV13111	Tipper, with winch, SWB
FV13112	Cargo, drop-side
FV13113	MT repair shop
FV13115	Recovery tractor
FV13116	L170 gun
FV13117	LCP, no 3
FV13118	BCP, no 2
FV13119	RCP, no 1
FV13120	Water tanker, 600gal

The full list of variants numbers almost 200, running from FV13101-FV13199 - a complete list appears in the editor's book 'Post-war British military vehicles'; ISBN 0-9525563-9-1.

of vehicles, the Bedford RL being designated the FV13100 series. Examples are given in the panel.

Whilst many of the RL's applications were similar to those called for in WW2, there were, too, some interesting new ones. Container bodies which weighed, empty, 500kg and were 2756x2235mm, with a height of 1854mm, were used for various applications from mobile offices to small workshops. Laird (Anglesey) Ltd, who once built MTBs and similar craft in the Menai Straits, produced some of these container bodies, with designations such as CB101, and these were, as with those from

Used by the Royal Marines and entering service about 1959-60, this 3-ton 4x4 GS cargo truck is fitted with a Marshall's body, and is also equipped for troop carrying with folding benches down the sides only - none down the centre as in the older style, more dedicated, troop carriers.

other manufacturers, like Marshall's of Cambridge, carried on the flatbed FV13136.

Another 'special' was the FV13142 Midge drone launch platform. The Midge was a pilotless reconnaissance aircraft pre-programmed with its course and exactly where to fire its cameras, the course usually being circular or elliptical to facilitate retrieval.

When 'Commercial Motor' first tested the RL they ran into one or two little teething problems, in spite of which they were well impressed with the vehicle. Advertising material for the RL made much of the ease of access to mechanical parts and the extent to which panels were removable for servicing. 'Commercial Motor' found this to be all too true as bits, notably the front bumper, came adrift whilst testing. There was also a transmission shaft failure, but they do admit that this only occurred in an 'extreme testing' phase.

They next tested an RL in July 1954, but this one was very special! Although Bedford did not offer a diesel option for the RL, a Perkins engine could be had in the S Type up until the time that Bedford introduced their own, in-house diesel. British Insulated Callender's Cables Ltd decided they needed a diesel unit - not for reasons of economy but because diesel fuel was seen as being less 'thievable' than petrol, on-site! A standard conversion kit was used to fit a Perkins R6 into an otherwise standard RL. No changes were required to the transmission but extra batteries were fitted to provide 24V, and some minor alterations

RLs and S Types come up for sale in all sorts of guises. This ex-RAF AVGAS bowser was in reasonable condition but the Carrimore tractor was 'rough'. Together with a replacement cab, the lot was knocked down for £1500 in 1998. Has it appeared in preservation yet?

to the exhaust pipe and the cooling system completed the picture. 'Commercial Motor' was very impressed with the result - their tests started with climbing a 1:2.74 loose-surfaced gradient which the truck managed 'on part-throttle only'; strange terminology as diesels do not actually have throttles!

Quoting direct from their test report, 'The most impressive part of the day's test came when the Bedford was taken on to the tank ground for cross-country trials. The surface here was deeply grooved and consisted for the most part of a sticky mixture of soft sand and loam interspersed with loose-bedded pools and small hillocks. During most of the half-hour spent under these conditions, the 4x4 ploughed its way steadily and relentlessly over the course after the fashion of the tanks with which it shared the ground. Second gear was used as much as low gear and it was not until the front differential housing became wedged on a ridge between two deep ruts that traction was lost. However, by shunting back and forth the vehicle got out on to firmer ground and outside assistance was not necessary'.

The RL continued in production until 1969, long after the S Type had been abandoned in favour of the TK. By this time a total of 73,135 RLs had been produced for civilian and military customers, worldwide. The next military Bedford was the MK, a four-wheel drive version of the TK which had proved to be so popular in the commercial market.

Tank Museum

Late model 3-ton 4x4 GS cargo truck comprehensively bogged down in loose sand - note the low position of the headlamps and the modified upper grille.

Post-War normal-control Bedfords

Having completed the story of the RL, this month Robert Coates looks at the normal-control Bedfords of the 'fifties and 'sixties

BETWEEN 1952 and their effective demise in 1986, Bedford produced three ranges of normal-control, or bonnetted, trucks. In chronological order, these were known as the A Type, D Type and J Type.

The A Type was introduced at the 1952 Commercial Motor Show for the 1953 model year, and was the intended replacement for the K, M and O Types which had been introduced before the War. By this time, Bedford was producing around 40,000 vehicles a year, about half of which were for export. Production, of all types, during 1952 was 43,739 and by 1954 production had topped 58,000 for the first time. The A Type was produced in 25-30cwt up to 6 ton, rigid, specification, or up to 8 tons as a Bedford-Scammell artic, until 1957.

The smallest, the A2, was a general-purpose chassis with a wide range of applications and, whilst it could readily be used for light truck work, its real value lay in its ride characteristics which made it suitable for pick-ups, medium vans, ambulances and crew-buses. At the top of the range, was the A5 model, with long- or short-wheelbase options, available as chassis only, chassis/cab or drop-side lorry, and with an optional diesel engine.

The D Type, which was only available

Used for carrying explosives - probably torpedoes - this fixed-side body was built by Edbro and fitted to a diesel-engined J5LC1 chassis around 1959-60. Various modifications have been necessary in its explosives role: the route for the exhaust pipe, headlamp guards, and a fire-screen extending well below the cab floor, to protect the driver.

Royal Navy - Crown Copyright

during 1957 and 1958, replaced the A Type and covered the weight range 30cwt to 6 tons, with a diesel engine option at the higher weights. It was introduced concurrently with the C Type, a very similar-looking forward-control lorry for smaller payloads than the S Type.

The J Types, often known as TJs, were introduced in 1958 and replaced both the A and D Types. These were available for commercial payloads from 25cwt up to 7 tons, representing gross weights of 3.35 tons - the J1 - up to 10.75 tons with the J6. All retained petrol-engine options

Henrik Clausen

Danish Army J6 fitted with a house-type shelter carried inside the cargo body. The J6 entered service with the Danes in 1962.

Henrik Clausen

although the actual engines on offer differed as gross vehicle weights (GVW) increased. The favoured chassis, at home and abroad, seems to have been the J5, for gross weights up to 9.7 tons, although J6s featured in, for example, the Danish Army's fleet. On both models there was a choice of wheelbase, and the engine options were either the 300in³ (4916cc) petrol or the Bedford 330in³ (5407cc) diesel.

Four-wheel drive versions for 30cwt working, based on the J5, were exhibited at FVRDE in the 'sixties, as development projects 'to assess their suitability for military work'. Versions were seen with both all-steel and with wooden bodies, earlier models - listed as J5S - having the 300in³ engine, later ones being shown with the 330in³ multi-fuel unit. This ensured an excellent power-to-weight ratio and, allegedly, enabled the vehicles to cope with gradients of 1:2. They were otherwise much the same as the standard commercial offerings except for their larger wheels and tyres and uprated suspension. Although it is believed that very small numbers were exported, none entered service with the British Army mainly because of the withdrawal of requirements for vehicles at this weight.

The similarities between the three

A crane-equipped cargo-bodied Bedford J6 in service with the Danish Army.

Danish Army Bedford A2C fitted with an interesting low-sided locally-built cargo body. All Danish Army Bedfords of this period were delivered in 'knocked-down' form and were assembled by the GM factory in Copenhagen.

Henrik Teller

normal-control ranges outnumber the differences, so to describe one is to describe all three. In all three ranges, an all-steel welded cab - new, for Bedford - was mounted as a single assembly with the wings and all the front-end sheet metal. It had a three-point rubber mounting designed to 'defy the roughest rough track' and, indeed, was well proved in export markets. Much attention was given to insulation: for heat-proofing, the roof, back and door-panels were double skinned and, for sound-proofing, the dash, toe-boards, floor and engine cowl were heavily insulated to reduce drumming and other mechanical noise as well as cutting out engine heat. Good as this may have been, it cannot be denied that, with the diesel option, it would have been difficult to fall asleep at the wheel! Draught-proofing and an element of dust-proofing were taken care of by sponge rubber on the doors, supplemented by tubular rubber weather strips round the door apertures; rubber 'boots' were also provided on the driving controls.

Signs that driver comfort were beginning to play a part in the design brief appeared in the form of such luxuries as a cab heater/demister, ash-tray, glove-box and... wait for it, provision for a radio! And maintenance fitters had not been forgotten, either; witness the ease with which the engine and other parts could be worked upon. Open the counter-sprung alligator bonnet lid and there was oodles of room all round the engine to work on it - so much so that it was possible for fitters to sit on either wing and lean forward into the engine compartment.

A petrol engine option was available for all three ranges, the engine in question being the ëExtra-Dutyí version of the old 28HP war-time unit in various states of tune. Introduced in 1950, it was a very popular engine which, even by the time the A Type was launched, had established a good reputation, world-wide. It developed 76bhp at 3200rpm in the smaller models and 84bhp at 3100rpm for the larger ones; torque was around 170 lbf/ft at 1000rpm.

The diesel option was the six-cylinder Perkins P6V which, at 4728cc, developed a shade less power (83 bhp) but a useful 20% extra torque, available over a wide rev-band. This engine, however, required a heavier clutch, stronger half-shafts in the rear axle and an exhauster for the vacuum-servo brakes and windscreen wipers. In mid-1956 the diesel option was extended to the 2/3 tonners and 25/35cwt models and, in 1957, Bedford introduced their own 'oiler', a 300in³, six-cylinder unit developing 97bhp at 2800rpm with an impressive 200 lbf/ft of torque available down as low as 800rpm.

Gearboxes were pretty straightforward affairs, with four forward and one reverse gear and synchromesh on the top three - a new departure for Bedford even though Vauxhall cars were amongst the first to adopt synchromesh. The gear-lever was cranked to ensure that the centre passenger had plenty of leg-room, but this did not prevent a sharp crack on the knee when a third-to-second change was needed in a hurry! Overall gearing was altered as it progressed through the weight range, by having different final-drive ratios available in the hypoid rear-axle - another new feature for Bedfords. Some of the larger models also came with an Eaton two-speed axle option.

In appearance, all three ranges were very similar and, if there were still enough of them around, they could easily be confused with each other. They could also fairly easily be confused with a number of other contemporary vehicles - both Ford (in the form of the K500, K600, etc) and Austin (with their normal-control Type 503 5-tonner) had similar-looking models available and even Commer, later, had an 8-ton rigid which had broadly similar lines; there was also a striking resemblance to the 1948 Chevrolet at the lower end of the weight range.

So, for the 'spotter', what are the distinguishing marks? Ford, Austin,

3-tonne cargo-bodied Bedford A5 of the Danish Army. *Henrik Teller*

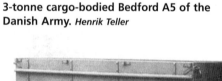

Photographed in the late 'nineties in Kenya, and still looking like new, a J6 with 'local' bodywork. This one is slightly unusual for its modest colour scheme - it is not unusual, in Africa and Asia, to see lorries painted in gaudy colour schemes and decorated with much paraphernalia.

Trevor Tydeman

Two special types of pantechnicon were built for the Navy by Papworth Industries around 1959-60 on a Bedford J5LC2 chassis. One was a standard pantechnicon but the other was a cut-down, or 'low-arch' version which was used for access to premises with restricted height. One drawback of this design was that, every time any really serious mechanical work was needed, the Luton body had to be removed. *Royal Navy - Crown Copyright*

Commer and Chevrolet can fairly quickly be eliminated by their respective badges, quite apart from various more-or-less subtle differences, but the others in the Bedford range are slightly more difficult.

The original A Types, dating from 1953, had their side-lamps incorporated in a decorative wing flash, a smooth dome to the bonnet and horizontal grille-bars for the radiator. In 1956 the sidelights were moved to the top of the wings and a hollow hump down the centre of the bonnet was introduced. Confusingly, the D Types adopted this bonnet in 1957, for the heavier models (4, 5 and 6 ton) but with the addition of a horizontal chrome styling strip above the radiator grille, whilst the lighter middleweights retained the 1956 cab front.

The TJs, introduced in 1958, had vertical grille slats for the radiator, and headlamp 'eyebrows' up to 4 tons, with horizontal grille slats for the heavier models, distinguishable from the As and the Ds by extending over a greater width and being interrupted by two vertical pieces. They also had a one-piece, curved windscreen compared with the A and D Types' divided screen. Even so, taken overall, it's not easy to tell one from the other. The J Types were by far the most plentiful and remained in production by Bedford and their successors, although in much reduced quantities, and for export markets only, for many years. With Bedford now all but disappeared, it seems strange that in 1969, when the TJ was still very much a going concern, they sold 21,273 commercial trucks and buses taking no less than 24% of the total market as well as 34,381 light vans - not a record but a very respectable figure. In fact, between 1959 and 1969 Bedford sold over a million vehicles and was not just Britain's, but the world's, largest exporter of trucks.

Very few were taken up by the British Armed Forces, except the Royal Navy, by whose kind permission some of the accompanying photos are reproduced. Because of its excellent ride characteristics, the A Type was used as a four-stretcher ambulance with bodies by various makers. It was rare to find a D Type in 'military' service - indeed it was rare to find a D Type! However, one rather unusual rig included a flight safety caravan which was purpose built at the Navy's Chatham yard and towed by a D Type. It was used for training and could be opened out to some 20-feet wide. The whole thing was fully self-contained, the sides simply being slid into the main body before moving. All supporting and loose bits were stowed inside or on the towing vehicle. A similar principle was employed for other specialist trailers for exhibition work and with the Clearance Diving Display Team.

But it was the J Type which was used in the largest numbers - albeit still quite small compared with the forward-control types available. The RN used them as general-purpose lorries, special 'explosives' vehicles, cesspool emptiers, and so on, but no evidence can be found of the British Army using them in any role whatsoever. However, a number of foreign armies used them for training and for GS Cargo applications - and not just in Africa.

There will be more to say about J Types when Bedford's successor, AWD Limited, comes up for examination.

In 1966, FVRDE trialled a second J5-based all-wheel drive vehicle, this time fitted with a wooden platform body designed to carry a standard 1-ton shelter container.

This all-wheel drive steel pick-up bodied J5S variant was trialled at FVRDE in the early 'sixties.

Bedford TK and M

The Bedford story continues and this month Robert Coates looks at the introduction of the TK and M models in 1960

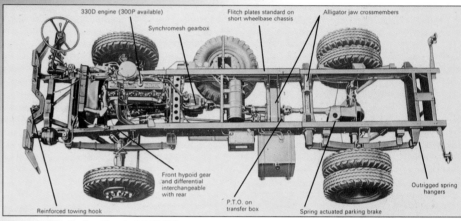

Chassis details for the 4x4 M1120.

WHEN Bedford announced the TK to civilian transport operators in September 1960, it was hailed with wildly enthusiastic epithets - 'the great leap forward', 'the first truly modern truck' and various other expressions of approval and this writer well remembers the sheer exhilaration of driving one for the first time. The TK was revolutionary in many ways: the cab was well forward - ahead even of the front wheels - with a short, business-like gear lever, air-brakes which sounded like air-brakes - not really new in themselves, but, in some indefinable way, different. The main thing seemed to be that it drove like a proper grown-up lorry and everything about it seemed... just wonderful, especially when compared with offerings from the likes of Austin, Morris, Ford and others. Although, to be fair, Ford were not that far behind with their rough old D Type (in which your intrepid reporter took his Class 1 HGV).

The TK was introduced at 7½ tons (model KC, later re-designated TK750) with successive announcements soon taking the range up into heavier weights right up to the, then, maximum for a two-axle

Bedford M4×4

Civilian brochure for the 4x4 M1120, dating from 1970, showing the two wheelbase lengths.

rigid vehicle of 16 tons gross (model KM, re-designated as the TK1630): there were also tractor units taking the gross train weight up to over 19 tons (as the KG or TK1930). Some operators had six- and even eight-wheeled conversions made for specific purposes, the breweries being particularly active in this sphere with both conventional and 'Chinese' sixes – but no 'eights'. In fact, only about a dozen or so 'eight leggers' were ever produced but neither sixes nor eights (from Bedford) figured in military fleets at this time.

TKs were available with a choice of petrol or diesel engines right up to 10 tons gross. At the lower end of the weight range, the diesel was a 200in³ unit which was, in effect, a four-cylinder version of the six-cylinder 300 engine which had been available since 1957, and which was an option on all

vehicles above 5-tons payload. Whilst it was a very simple 'lump', it was not without its problems. It used up gaskets as if there was no tomorrow, as well as having several other little idiosyncrasies and, by the time it had aged a little, it became a 'noisy old knocker'. It could also be a recalcitrant starter in cold weather although this was nothing that could not be fixed by a few squirts of Cold-Start or a flaming rag stuffed into the air-intake! Flaming rags were sometimes available from the little bonfire which had been lit beneath the fuel tank to thaw out waxed fuel!

The Forces used TKs for just about every task imaginable: a typical Garrison Support squadron might be equipped with 20-odd TK 4-tonners for general service, cargo, with another half-dozen as pantechnicons or for food delivery, plus a tractor unit for use with sundry semi-trailers and a TK (or, later, TL) Lacre road sweeper. It is not my intention to go into detail here about the TL model: suffice it to say that, late in the life of the TK, the range was given a fairly major, albeit inadequately-financed, face-lift which was designated TL, an unfortunate move which turned out to be a damp squib.

Another example of the degree to which the Army embraced the TK is given by the fact that its School of Mechanical Transport had a fleet of over 180 of them for HGV training purposes and, just about everywhere you looked, you'd see one or other variant of the range in use. Bedford produced their half-millionth TK in 1978 so, it seems, their old slogan, 'You see them everywhere,' remained true.

But we are getting ahead of ourselves.

Model codes

When the TK range was first introduced, models were known by letter-pairs, for example, the smallest in the range, for five-and-a-half ton (gross) working, were known as the KB. This then progressed up through the range with KC, KD, KE etc, ultimately to KM which was the maximum gross weight rigid chassis for 16-ton working. This nomenclature was, however, changed to bring it a little more in line with the terminology used by other manufacturers who used, for example '1617' to denote 16 tons with 170bhp engine. Bedford, however, didn't quite get the idea right so remained unique with their designations which seem to be all over the place. Examples are TK1630 representing 16 tons with the 300in³ engine but TK1260 representing 12 tons with a 60-series engine.

Old and new model designations

GVW/GTW (tonnes)	Chassis designation: old	new
5.690	KB	TK570
7.490	KC	TK750
7.37/8.64	KD	TK860*
11.97/12.53	KD	TK60 6x2*
10.0	KE	TK1000
15.23	KE	TK1000 6x2
16.26	KFA	TK1630 tractor
12.55	KG	TK1260
14.73	KG	TK1260 6x2**
19.31	KGA	TK1930 tractor
14.74	KH	TK1470
16.26	KM	TK1630

* different wheelbases; ** twin-steer

Passenger's eye view of the driving position in the M1120 4x4 which differed little, if at all, from the military MK.

circles. But the story does not end there; in fact, it has hardly begun as far as the Army is concerned. In the early 'sixties, more-or-less at the same time as the TK was announced, the Army issued a specification for a new off-road load carrier. This dictated strict weight limits and called for a vehicle which could carry four tonnes whilst meeting the Army's 'medium mobility' requirements. By the mid-sixties, a three-sided contest had ensued, between Austin, Bedford and Commer.

Bedford offered various development vehicles, mainly based on the KF model and with various types of bodywork, including water and refuelling tankers. Development vehicles were also offered in four-wheel drive format, with the model designation 'R Mk 2', these including a couple of 3-5 ton cargo models with an extra-wide track (to cope with top-heavy loads) and a choice of suspension options.

Amongst these was what was to become the M Type for civilian usage and the MK for the military. It was first exhibited as a development vehicle in 1966 and was the one with which Bedford emerged the winner. The M Type, or M1120 4x4, was available with single or twin rear wheels, a factor which dictated their UK plating and design weights. With singles, GVW was restricted to 9650kg or 9.5 tons whilst, with twins, GVW could be 11,180kg or 11.0 tons, all on wheelbase options of 138in or 156in. The gearbox was a four-speed (plus reverse) wide-ratio unit with a two-speed constant-mesh transfer box for low-ratio and four-wheel drive. It was a lovely vehicle and was quickly snapped up by local authorities for gritting and other off-road work, by utilities and by fire brigades as well as 'common or garden' off-road operators.

'Commercial Motor' magazine tested the M Type loaded with just under 3.75 tons of test weights (equivalent to 9.4 tons gross) at the Bagshot Heath proving grounds

Part of the Shopland collection of military vehicles and militaria which is dominated by AEC Mandators; these beauties are a mere side-show! The little sign-written lorry on the left is an ex-RN vehicle with a late (TL style) cab.

The RAF used TKs in a variety of roles, as did the Royal Navy. In sailors' livery we find such applications as general cargo, refuellers, artic tractors and, in fact, any other road-going role that might crop up. This is very much in line with the Navy's policy of buying their vehicles 'off-the-shelf' as they rarely have a need for off-road transport and, when they do, they can turn either to the Royal Marines or the Army to meet their needs. The Army, on the other hand, used fewer standard commercial chassis and used the designation CL, as in 'truck, 4-tonne, Bedford TK, CL', to represent the fact that the vehicle was a normal, commercial vehicle, as distinct from a 'ruggedised' military one.

So much, then, for the 'ubiquitous TK' as it came to be known in some

Bedford brochure for the M Type from 1976.

The go-anywhere truck that meets every demand

Built to meet exacting military needs originally, there's no stopping this extra-tough Bedford 4 x 4 M1120 model. Whatever the task or terrain, its rugged, flexible chassis meets any and every demand.

This very attractive TK mobile control room is still in service on the occasional fly-in days held at the Brooklands Museum at Weybridge in Surrey. Photographed on one of the Museum's Commercial Vehicle days, it was being used, to very good effect, as a static public-address system vehicle.

which consist essentially of a series of consecutive gradients at around 1:3 and 1:4, the most severe being 1:2.75. The M Type took all these with no trouble as well as managing a restart on a 1:3 slope. It was then put through its paces on the tracks at the Military Vehicles and Engineering Establishment (the new name for what had been, for many years, the FVRDE) at Chobham where braking and acceleration checks produced first-class results, whilst fuel consumption on roads varied between 9.4 and 14.2mpg depending upon speed and conditions.

On the 'rough road' track the suspension showed up very well with speeds of over 30mph

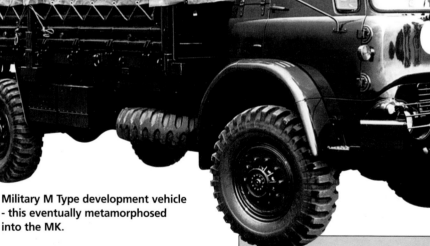

being maintained without discomfort, the M accepting 'a considerable amount of punishment without a murmur'. The deep transverse ruts, bumps and humps of the 'cross-country' section called for more caution but, although the ground was well churned up, there was 'never a sign that traction would be lost and, when run fairly briskly through deep water, less than a cupful got into the cab'.

The test was completed on what the tester described as the worst pavé he had ever encountered. The Bedford, he reported, did very well to complete a run at between 18 and 20mph and 'at this sort of speed was never out of control'. Looking back at the road test report of the R Type it is clear that the M did very much better, this being not just that higher speeds were possible but that nothing came adrift!

In short, the tester found the M Type a considerable improvement on the old RL and clearly liked driving it - particularly as there was a big improvement in visibility - less than 10 feet of the road in front of the driver being obscured, compared with almost 20 feet on the R type. It also had a much better trim than the RL.

With some modifications the M Type became the vehicle which the Army selected, a subject we shall explore in greater detail next month.

Military M Type development vehicle - this eventually metamorphosed into the MK.

Dating from 1966/69, this KFSC5 was primarily for the carriage of ammunition, but was also fitted with a towing hook. Always Welding Limited, of Aldershot provided the body which allowed a 7-ton payload within its GVW of nearly 11 tons. This vehicle is slightly unusual in that the tilt hoops are inside, thus allowing the dropsides to be used with the tilt still in position - a useful feature when handling ammunition - like missiles - which might be secret. Later models had a more-carefully protected exhaust system, the Regulations for explosives vehicles being very strict although, strangely, not as strict as for petroleum.

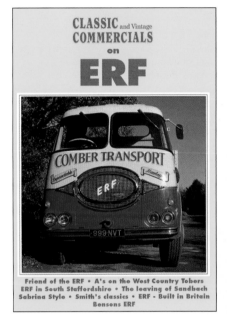

Bedford MK and MJ

Robert Coates continues his examination of Bedford military vehicles by looking at the MK and MJ models which started to enter service in the 'seventies

L AST month we saw how the civilian M Type, the M1120 4x4, suitably modified, became the Army's choice for its new four-tonner, Bedford having won the three-sided contest against Austin and Commer. Various development versions were exhibited during the 'sixties, and these culminated in the RK which was, ultimately, almost identical to the M Type. Most of the differences were confined to the electrical and fuel systems, and the fitting of additional equipment on the military version, such as a winch, trailer-brake connection, hooks, and so on.

According to the Army Handbook, 'the 4 tonne cargo vehicle is an all-wheel drive logistic vehicle with a 4 tonne payload and is designed to carry 6 Unit Load Containers or pallets. The vehicle is based on proved commercial components with special military features incorporated. It can be supplied with or without a 4 tonne capacity winch.'

After acceptance by the military the vehicle was designated 'MK' and was assigned the series FV13800. The first contract was placed in 1968 for 2000 vehicles, and these started entering service in 1970/71. The Army had decided that it would standardise on a single fuel, and the MK was the first general logistic support vehicle with a diesel engine, although this ensured that it was slower than the 'old' petrol-engined RL which it replaced.

In appearance, MKs differed little from TKs except for higher ground clearance and different tyres which make them look very

Definitive VB2025-3100 (formerly FV13801) steel-bodied cargo MJ; if fitted with winch, it would be VB2050-3100 (FV13803); in left-hand drive form, VB2025-8100 (FV13802) or VB2050-8100 (FV13804).

rugged and business-like and, whilst its cab looked much larger than its predecessor, it was actually less than three inches longer. Fully metricated now, the vehicle was 6.579m long; a fraction over 2.5m high to the top of the cab and, to the top of the tarpaulin, just over 3.4m; the front track was 2.05m, and the rear, 2.03m, making it just under 2.5m wide. Load area on the 'standard' version measured 4.28x2.01m. Loaded weight was, initially, stated as 9650kg (9.48 tons) although different tyres - and different sources of information - give different gross weights.

Maximum road speed was supposed to be 45-46mph, but just how meaningless such figures can be is well known! Range was 350 miles from a 33-gallon fuel tank, representing fuel consumption of something like 10-11mpg.

The engine was, basically, Bedford's own six-cylinder, in-line, 330in³ (5420cc), four-stroke, direct injection, push-rod operated overhead-valve, side-cam diesel - but with a difference. It was a 'multi-fuel' engine, capable of running on DERV, petrol and certain types of aviation fuel such as AVTUR and AVGAS. It was said, at the time, that it would also run on melted peanut butter but documentary evidence of this has been 'hard to come by'! Running on DERV, it developed about 106bhp at 2800 rpm.

Drive was through a four-speed, synchromesh gearbox and single dry-plate clutch, through a single propeller shaft to what was then a new design of transfer box, incorporating a clutch and interlock, and providing for selection of two- and four-wheel drive with the 'high' (1:1) and 'low' (2:1) ratios: with the old R type, four-wheel drive could be engaged only when in 'low'.

The MK also had a new

One of the MK development models carrying a steel drop-side body similar to that used on the RL - similar bodies were fitted to the Commer and Austin submissions.

This shows another of the development MKs, this time with a flat-platform body carrying a CB305 removable shelter - these shelters were also carried on RL chassis.

braking installation - air-hydraulic with a Clayton-Dewandre combined tandem master cylinder and dual air actuator being the main components. Independent circuits for each axle fed air to the unit so that, in the event of one of the circuits failing, there was still half braking left on all wheels: the handbrake on military versions was mechanical. Single 12.00x20 wheels and tyres were fitted all round giving a gross rating of 9.3 tons. The MK had a fording depth of 760mm, but this has to be slightly theoretical since, a) it's difficult to be that precise with fording depths - even if only for the bow-wave effect, and b) who's going to get out to measure it anyway?

As with the QL and RL which preceded the MK, many roles were fulfilled by a single basic vehicle design. With the QL, each role that required a different body had its own vehicle; in other words they were purpose-dedicated, even if the purpose was General Service - Cargo. This pattern continued with the RL but the last few hundred RLs broke the mould. These were supplied as flat platform lorries onto which could be lifted a variety of special-purpose, containerised, bodies. This was

A line of MKs parked up at Leavesley's of Alrewas, Staffs, the NATO vehicle-disposal specialists. Leavesley's recondition all the vehicles they sell, only buying 'the cream' of the pack at auction as they supply organisations like Christian Aid and other relief charities. They also dispose of a fair quantity of vehicles from other countries... well worth a visit!

hardly innovative as the commercial sector had been unitised - and palletised - for some time, although the idea had not developed to the stage that it has today. The idea, though, was taken up with a vengeance with the introduction of the MK as it gave great flexibility and economy of operation.

The 'standard' version was the 4 tonne drop-side general service truck, the Army's standard task vehicle, asset code VB2025 which, towards the end of its service life - mainly after the TM was introduced - was 'demoted' to being a domestic vehicle, or runabout. Note that, by this time, the Army had dropped the old FV classifications and replaced them with 'asset codes', following assault from all quarters by various management consultancies and being 'more in line with modern thinking'. Asset codes remain - theoretically - 'classified'. However, to continue, VB2026 was the 'winterised' version which meant that it had a decent cab-heater and a radiator muff, initially fitted by unit workshops, but latterly by Bedford. VB2050

was the winch-equipped version designed for self-recovery or recovery of vehicles of similar or smaller size. These are readily identified by front and rear winch sheaves and extra boxes under the body for equipment which reduced payload to 3½ tons with a steel body or 4 tons with aluminium.

VB2091 was the flat-platform version and VB2094 the same thing with an Atlas crane behind the cab, the whole outfit being referred to as a CALM (crane appliance, lorry mounted). VB2204 was the bulk fuel version on which the 'bulk' was carried in pallet-sized tanks known as UBREs (unit bulk re-fuelling equipment) and dispensed from PODs (petrol and oil dispensers) of which each vehicle had to carry just one. The idea was taken up, if not developed simultaneously, by the brewing industry for delivering bulk beer (180 gallons at a time) to appropriately-equipped cellars.

The MK was replaced in 1982 - although some may have entered service as early as 1981 - by an improved version of what was, essentially, the same vehicle with a different engine. Known as the MJ it is virtually impossible, externally, to tell the difference between the old and the new - unless you are 'in to' registration marks, in

Lovely large-scale model of the MK produced at MWEE, Chertsey presumably to demonstrate the soon-to-be standard 4-tonne cargo body to the user arms.

'Arcticisation'

Some vehicles had special preparations for use in arctic conditions, notably in Norway where much arctic training is carried out. These included arrangements for improved cab-heating, consisting of tubes which ran round the cab interior circulating hot air from the engine compartment to form an efficient and cheap form of heating. Also, Velcro strips, fitted beneath the windscreen and side windows, secure fabric screens which roll down from the roof at night to prevent the glass become deeply encrusted with frost - saves a lot of scraping on a cold morning!

General view of an 'articised' cab on an MJ; Velcro strips along the waistline secure the roll-down screens at night to prevent the windows from frosting up. These MJs were, apparently, the most reliable vehicles that the Royal Marines ever had in Norway.

An MJ of the Royal Anglian Regiment photographed at West Bergholt in 1995. This vehicle is something of a puzzle - it sports an AWD badge, yet the cab is unmistakably of the old 'TK' type whereas AWD's cabs were of the later 'TL' style. Maybe it's an early AWD and they were just using up old pressings. Can anyone shed more light on this?

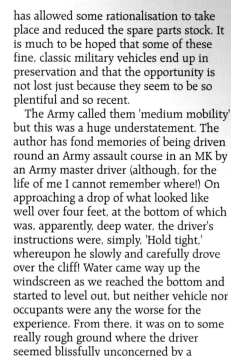

A winch equipped MJ, 'arcticised' and fitted with Boughton recovery equipment.

which case, if it has a letter pair before 'K-something', it's an MK and if it's 'K-something', it's an MJ! The improved engine was the 330D Turbo, a turbocharged version of the old 330 and a delightful engine to drive, being considerably faster than the older, multi-fuel engine. Some examples of the variants available with the MJ 4-tonne 4x4 are shown in the panel.

Production figures for these two models have been very hard to ascertain but, by combing information from different sources, the best estimate seems to be that, by the end of 1977, some 11,700 vehicles

had been built, 1943 of those being in 1977 alone. In 1983, another 726 vehicles were added to the total and, in 1985 a further 3094 came on stream. As for the final total, or what happened in the intervening years, the best estimate (from a Danish website!) seems to be about 50,000 of the MK and MJ types combined. At the time of writing, there are 5902 MJs still in service, some of which are being refurbished in preference to retaining Leyland-DAFs from the 'nineties.

Casting, or disposal, of the MK started in about October 1994 and, by the time this appears in print, all will have gone. This

has allowed some rationalisation to take place and reduced the spare parts stock. It is much to be hoped that some of these fine, classic military vehicles end up in preservation and that the opportunity is not lost just because they seem to be so plentiful and so recent.

The Army called them 'medium mobility' but this was a huge understatement. The author has fond memories of being driven round an Army assault course in an MK by an Army master driver (although, for the life of me I cannot remember where!) On approaching a drop of what looked like well over four feet, at the bottom of which was, apparently, deep water, the driver's instructions were, simply, 'Hold tight,' whereupon he slowly and carefully drove over the cliff! Water came way up the windscreen as we reached the bottom and started to level out, but neither vehicle nor occupants were any the worse for the experience. From there, it was on to some really rough ground where the driver seemed blissfully unconcerned by a slightly disconcerting sound from the engine compartment. It was only the cooling-fan blades striking the chassis which was so supple, strong and flexible that it could contort to a huge degree without damage - or so he told me.

They don't make 'em like that any more!

A pair of MJ UBREs.

BEDFORD'S TM FOUR-FOURS AND SIX-SIXES

Robert Coates takes a look at Bedford's military swansong - the big TM

The TM was the last truck range Bedford ever produced - it was not destined to succeed. Bedford's strengths in the commercial sector had always been in robust, reasonably-priced middle-weight lorries and, in military markets, they went almost unchallenged in their chosen weight range.

The two-millionth Bedford was produced at the close of the 'sixties, and the three-millionth 10 years later: of these, two million had been trucks and buses, the remainder were vans. Like all vigorous enterprises, Bedford wanted more, but an old saying decrees that 'if you don't know where you're going, any road will take you there' and, in the mid-seventies, there were signs that Bedford had lost its way. Attempts to enter the heavy truck market, with 'beefed-up' 28-ton - and bigger - KMs met with little success. Bedford had made its name with rugged middle-weight rigids where they were world beaters, and it seemed that this was their niche.

In an attempt to produce what might be seen as a 'world truck', in the early 'seventies, Bedford developed the TM. Launched onto the UK market in 1974, the TM gave operators plenty to choose from - maybe too much.

The range included trucks at almost any weight between 15 and 42 tonnes gross. There were three different cabs - D, F and H - the narrowest of which, the tilting D, had at one stage been intended as a replacement for the ageing TK. It was a pity they didn't use it because the non-tilting TL cab, which was used instead, was a big disappointment to Bedford's traditional buyers. The F cab was a wider version of the D, mainly to take the extra width of the two-stroke Detroit-Diesel 6V engine, and the H cab was much the same as the F, but with a sleeper.

The Detroit engine was the TM's downfall. Unfamiliar to, and unpopular with, British drivers, many felt that it was arrogant of General Motors to foist 'this foreign contraption' onto the UK market. The engine was considered to be too noisy, and too high-revving - the total antithesis of the 'legendary' Gardner.

Meanwhile, back in 1970, the Army had called for a new 8-tonner with an expected into-service date of around 1980. Foden, Leyland and Bedford all competed, but Bedford carried the day. An initial order for 2000 TM trucks was placed and these started to enter service in 1978, gradually replacing some of the existing 4-tonne Bedford MK/MJ, and the 10-tonne AEC Militant Mk 1 medium-mobility trucks.

But this was a TM with a difference!

Designated the 4-4 8000kg truck, it was the result of lengthy testing and modification to the standard civilian-specification vehicle. It had four-wheel drive and, in place of the Detroit 'lump', was powered by the Bedford 500 over-head valve engine, a development of the '70 Series' 466in³ unit which had been popular in commercial fleets but had not figured in any military specifications. Unusually, when increasing an engine's capacity, Bedford chose to lengthen the stroke, rather than increase the bore. This meant a new crankshaft and changes to various other 'bottom end' dimensions but, it remained typical of Bedford engines which had always been of the 'long-stroke' variety, and was strong on torque. The 500 was a really super engine with bags of power from its 8198 cc - 202bhp gross or about 151 net. It was smooth and quiet - a lovely piece of work!

Other mechanical features of interest are the twin dry-plate clutch, compared with the single on the MJ; a 6F1R gearbox, very similar to that used on the commercial KM; and good, old fashioned semi-elliptical springs with telescopic shockers all round.

These TM 6-6 general-service trucks have removable drop-sides. Together with many others from the Royal Marines, they were used on Operation Haven in 1991 as a shuttle service from the mountains ferrying refugee Kurds from Saddam Hussein. They are said to be unstoppable and excellent off-road.

Like most army vehicles, the TM was a pleasure to drive. Visibility was good; cab comfort, especially considering that they were for on- and off-road use, was good; and controls were simple and easy-to-use. The control for selecting four-wheel drive and low-ratio gears was very different from older applications where the driver had to pull lots of interesting levers. On the TM there was a large plastic hand-wheel on top of the engine cover which was simply turned so that the indicator pointed to the selected option. Not nearly so much fun, perhaps, but probably more foolproof.

In appearance, the TM was square and functional. It was 6.694m long (about 22 feet), just under 2.5m wide and nearly 3m to the top of the cab or 3.45m to the top of the tilt. It provided angles of approach and departure of 41° and 35° respectively, and could ford water of a touch over 750mm deep.

The 4-4 was available as a general-service (GS) cargo vehicle (asset code VB2390), with a loading-bed height compatible with the old 4-tonner, and was also available equipped with a winch (VB2392), or as what the Army describe as a

TM 4-4 8-tonne flat and GS - both these vehicles saw service in Iraq.

Possibly one of the very last GM Bedford TM 6-6s, dating from about 1986, with a GS flat platform body and ISO-compatible container on board. (Marshall's Limited)

CALM ('crane appliance, lorry mounted') (VB2394). Finally, on a shorter wheelbase, there was also a tipper (VB2404).

Later came the TM 6-6 which, with its 14,000kg payload capacity, was intended to replace the remainder of the AEC 'knockers' - the Militant Mk 1 - as well as the later Mk 3. The prototype was ready in late 1981, and the 6-6 shared much with its smaller 4-4 cousin. The 6-6 model range included a GS cargo vehicle (VB2478), plus a similar

14-tonne workshops 'LS ('Log Sup' or Logistics Support) Squadron Royal Marines. Inside the TM container bodies, mobile racking is installed in which engineering stores are held ready for deployment at a few moments' notice.

model with a centrally-mounted 10,000kg recovery winch (VB2490); like the 4-4, there was also a CALM variant (VB2491). The vehicles started to enter service in the latter part of the 'eighties and I well recall 'inspecting' (ie, clambering all over) one of the first batches to arrive at Aldershot, before they were painted in their 'DPM' disruptive pattern markings.

The Army welcomed the introduction of these two models with open arms - well, welcomed, anyway. Although it had, basically, the same dimensions as the old 4-tonner, it could carry twice the load, palletised or in unit load form so, 'at a stroke' the 4-4 doubled the uplift capability of many of the transport task troops to which it was assigned.

The basic vehicles have removable dropsides and a canopy, being rigged as flatbeds for carrying ammunition pallets or container bodies and, at least for the moment, will remain in service even with the advent of DROPS ('demountable rack off-load and pick-up system'). There are some sinister rumblings within the Defence Procurement Agency - and the Royal Logistic Corps - about the TM's eventual replacement which could well be American, and Oshkosh at that!

But, exciting as all this was, all was not well in the commercial-vehicle world. Demand for trucks had slumped during the 'eighties, and many long-established companies, in the UK and overseas, were in deep trouble. Leyland was in desperate straits and Foden wasn't much better. Even the US truck producers were feeling the

pinch, and General Motors, which had plants in many countries, but major ones in Britain and Germany, were feeling it more than most.

When it became clear that Leyland, which had absorbed huge sums of public money, had to be disposed of, General

TM 6-6 on proving trials ... (Marshall's Limited)

...and on tilt-tests. Much of this work is carried out at Chobham, in Surrey, at what was the FVRDE. Now available as a test site to 'selected authorised personnel' the author has spent many happy hours here testing load-restraint systems for the brewing industry - any excuse! (Marshall's Limited)

This TM 4-4 is one of the original batch of 2000 ordered by the Ministry of Defence following Bedford's success against Leyland and Foden opposition. It is fitted with a general service platform body, carrying a Marshall Matrix shelter equipped with a Geographic Support System for military survey which includes technical equipment to produce and print maps as well as overprinting operational information on existing maps. The '8 tonne' is seen here painted up in United Nations colours ready for shipment to Bosnia. *(Marshall's Limited)*

Motors showed interest in acquiring it. This, they argued, would enable them to effect economies of scale by closing down Opel in Germany and centralising their European truck production at Dunstable. They went as far as to say that, if they couldn't have

From October 1980, the TM4-4 was also available on the civilian market for operators requiring off-road capability. (Vauxhall Motors)

Leyland, they would have to close down Bedford. The Government of the day, in the form of Margaret Thatcher and Paul Channon, didn't believe them and, in order to keep the whole show in European hands, sold Leyland to DAF which, itself, went bust just a few months later.

General Motors were as good as their

word and pulled the rug on a, by now, much-weakened, Bedford which simply 'went down the tubes'. If only politicians would stick to what they're good at - whatever that is - and leave running businesses to people who know what they're doing! Bedford will go down in history as possibly the most prolific and successful truck (and bus and van) producer the world has ever seen, or is ever likely to.

The TM was the last complete commercial vehicle model range introduced by GM through their Vauxhall Motors subsidiary. It was a valiant try which was simply not sufficiently successful. Two things counted against it. Firstly, it was off to a bad start because high-revving two-strokes were unpopular with British lorry-drivers, and secondly, it consistently turned in disappointing fuel consumption figures. So, with neither drivers and operators in favour, it was doomed. Military contracts were nowhere near large enough to keep the Company afloat in anything like its existing form and without a substantial commercial 'base-load' there wasn't a hope.

Bedford press photograph of the GS-bodied 14-tonne TM 6-6. (Vauxhall Motors)

Or was there? Next month we look at how the Company was saved with TMs figuring quite boldly in the range offered by the new owners.

My thanks to the Commanding Officer - and many others - of the Royal Marines Logistic Regiment at Chivenor Barracks for their co-operation in obtaining some of these photographs. ▪

Pictured in 1978 at the International Air Fair, Bedford contrasts the military TM against the WW2 MW - hardly a fair comparison since the 8-tonne rating of the TM 4-4 is bound to make the 15cwt MW seem a little on the small side. (Vauxhall Motors)

BEDFORD AND AWD

In 1986, Bedford went into receivership - Robert Coates takes a look at the Company's subsequent rescue by AWD

Designated MTM 40-30, the 8x8 off-roader had a payload capacity of 27 tonnes - ideal for transporting 'light A' vehicles, as shown. This was, of course, a Multidrive product and had a Caterpillar/ZF driveline to transmit traction to all four axles. (AWD Limited)

Bedford called in the receivers in 1986, partly as a result of desperately-poor demand in the truck market, world-wide; partly because their traditional buyers had lost confidence after the disastrous introduction of the TL/TM ranges. But the main reason was political interference. Margaret Thatcher and Paul Channon thought they were the saviours of the European truck industry, and dealt Bedford a death-blow by not allowing their parent company, General Motors, to acquire British Leyland. This, together with the closure of Opel in Germany, would have allowed GM to concentrate their European activities at Dunstable and would have given them the economies of scale they needed in Europe.

Admittedly, some of Bedford's problems were of their own making. The 'new' TL range met nobody's expectations, being little more than a face-lifted TK, without even a tilt-cab. And the TM was disliked by commercial operators because of its Detroit Diesel two-stroke V6 engine, which was changed too late make any real difference. The relatively-modest orders for the conventionally-powered military variants, the 4-4 and the 6-6, were insufficient to save the Company.

However, all was not lost. The assets of Bedford were bought by David J B Brown - not the 'gear-boxes and Aston-Martin' David Brown, but another brilliant engineer and entrepreneur who owned a portfolio of successful engineering companies. He set up a new outfit which he called AWD Limited. The initials stand for All-Wheel Drive - a fair indication of his intentions, in

1990 brochure shot for the TL-cabbed MT which replaced the old MK/MJ. (AWD Limited)

AWD – BEDFORD TRUCKS

In addition to their range of civilian trucks which ran from 6500 to 32,500kg, AWD produced - or at least offered - three other ranges. The 'military' range consisted of the 17-tonne TM 4-4 with an 8.2 litre, 205bhp Perkins turbo-diesel and Spicer six-speed direct-top gearbox; two versions of the TM 30-30, at 30 tonnes as a 6x6, and at 41 tonnes as an 8x8, both with Caterpillar diesels and ZF 16-speed gearboxes; plus, at the top of the range, the TT1 20-40, a tank transporter for 44 tonnes with a Cummins engine and Fuller nine-speed gearbox.

An intermediate 'military/civilian' range offered four vehicles from 12 to 14.75 tonnes, known as the MT range (eg, MT12-16, etc), with Perkins engines and Spicer five-speed gearboxes.

Finally, the Multidrive range, which offered the MTL33-27 with a Cummins engine and Eaton nine-speed 'box, plus the MT55 and MTM40-30 with Caterpillar engines and ZF 16-speed gearboxes.

Multidrive produced all-wheel drive chassis, including artics. On acquiring Bedford, they lost no time in producing prototypes on the TM and TL chassis with power transmitted to the trailer axles. This enabled quite miraculous feats to be performed - like stopping on loose gravel, fully laden on a 1:4 gradient, and then reversing back up the slope!

Most of the Multidrives were fitted with rear-axle steering, too, and driving them was a weird experience. Trailer cut-in was almost eliminated, as the rear wheels tracked almost exactly with those of the tractor unit, but reversing was more difficult, requiring the driver to be alert to the slightest change in trailer direction.

which, it was hoped, military and other off-road vehicles would play a large part. He certainly had no intention of competing head-on with mass-producers like Ford and Leyland. His purchase, though, did not include the rights to use the name 'Bedford' except in very special circumstances, of which more later.

The new company sat comfortably alongside others in the Brown portfolio which included Artix, the world's leading manufacturer of articulated dump-trucks, and Brown Design Engineering which designed and manufactured Multidrive as well as a range of rough-terrain, materials-handling equipment. The intention was to 'build on strength', creating and developing niche markets. One obvious niche was in the military world, where AWD would seek to remain the principal UK supplier of trucks to the armed forces, whilst also enabling them to service other 'off-road' markets.

Exports - where Bedford always had been very strong - were another obvious niche. In some 'Third World' countries the word for a truck is 'Bedford', just as we refer to Hoover

Unusual to see tracked tyres on trailer axles, this 8x8 articulated tipper was demonstrated to, but not taken up by, the military authorities. It was a strange beast to drive! (AWD Limited)

agreement with General Motors only permitted use of the Bedford name in export markets outside Europe, (and on sales to the British government) as long as the AWD name appeared with it, and so they were badged 'AWD-Bedford'.

The third niche market was intended to be 'specialist vehicles' - those requiring features not compatible with volume production. Obvious targets were the once-loyal breweries, food distribution, and the municipal sectors.

carried the Bedford name. To Bedford enthusiasts it was incongruous to see vehicles like the 'Rascal', a Japanese-derived design with an engine of less than 1000cc, sporting such a grand name. Fortunately, it was not long before these small vans reverted to being called 'Vauxhall'.

By the end of 1988, AWD announced that turnover for their first 14 months of operation was £140 million, exports accounting for about 25% of this, and spares about 10%. The following year, they announced their intentions with regard to the three niche markets. Their plans included adding new models to take the range up to 425bhp and 44 tonnes GCW to cover all types of applications. This would have entailed discontinuing the use of Bedford engines in favour of Perkins Phaser, Cummins B and C, and Caterpillar diesels.

For military applications, there would be a full range of vehicles, in 4x4, 6x6 and 8x8 configurations, with power units ranging from 100-400bhp, GVWs from 10-40 tonnes, and GCWs from 20-120 tonnes. Finally, there would be a range of heavy-duty, all-terrain trucks to include 6x4, 6x6, 8x6 and 10x8 configurations, up to 68 tonnes GVW and 80 tonnes GTW with 425bhp engines.

By 1991, however, turnover had dropped to around £60 million, with exports accounting for 80% - a figure which was boosted by an order for 2000 TLs from

It wasn't long before AWD produced what was, in effect, the successor to the MJ, using the TL cab, and offered this logistics vehicle at 10, 12 and 14.75 tonnes GVW. It had a hydraulically-tilted cab and a variety of Perkins engines available, all with Spicer five-speed overdrive and two-speed transfer 'boxes. (AWD Limited)

and Biro. These markets need a relatively 'low-spec' vehicle which can be serviced standing on one's head in a swamp. The model favoured was the normal-control J-Type (see CMV, January 2003). The

Use of the Bedford name in these markets was, however, not permitted. GM obviously felt there was still 'life' left in the name for their own use and, indeed, light and medium vans produced at the car plant

Zimbabwe. Other contracts, for up to 4000 vehicles, were delayed by politics and bureaucracy, leaving AWD with uneconomic small orders in the home market. There was almost no expenditure on promotion or advertising, and the introduction of new ideas was delayed because of the efforts being devoted to export business and Type Approval for the home market.

Even all AWD's expertise was not enough to ensure survival. From a figure of 6000, production fell to 4385 in 1989 and 2398 in 1990, recovering to 3017 in 1991. But, in 1992, only 32 trucks had been produced by mid-year bringing their total production to 15,832 vehicles from mid-1987 to the end of 1992. With only a handful of vehicles produced in the final year, the receivers were in again.

With so much seeming to be going for them, what went wrong?

A leader in 'Transport Engineer' magazine in July 1992 criticised the 'typical vacillation' of the General Motors' committee system which had allowed a year to elapse between closing-down Bedford and selling it. In the interim, world-marketing momentum was lost and much of the distributor chain broken up. Also, of course, AWD had only been granted partial rights to use the Bedford brand name: rights to the cash-generating supply of spares being retained by GM who gave no undertaking not to compete with Isuzu imports - or even assembly - in the future. The failure to win the contest against Leyland and Volvo for the Army's 4-tonne 4x4 replacement was also undoubtedly a significant factor.

Added to these problems, demand for trucks was still at a very low ebb, AWD was faced with a crash-programme of Type Approval and, even with their stalwart efforts in export markets, they just could not generate the volume. Attempts were made to consolidate some of the Dunstable site, parts of which were quite modern whilst others were pretty antiquated. Even this, perfectly normal, rationalisation was mis-read by the market who feared that it signalled the start of asset-stripping and an eventual pull-out. AWD certainly had no intentions

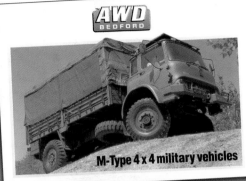

This 1988 brochure, clearly badged 'AWD-Bedford', shows the old MK/MJ which was initially offered as the 'M Type' with the original cab. (AWD Limited)

M-Type 4 x 4 military vehicles

to retrench. The re-organised plant had capacity to produce 30,000 vehicles per shift, per year, far in excess of current requirements. Bedford, in their last year of GM ownership, had produced just under 5000 vehicles; AWD, in their first full year of operations, had managed to increase this to 6000.

There was also a view that AWD had been too cautious in exploring more niche markets - midi-buses, a lightweight eight-wheeler, and modifications to the (commercial) TM - including a different power unit. Whilst not large, these might have generated sales at the margin but, as ever, it's easy to be wise after the event.

The receivers were to find that the mood of potential buyers was less than buoyant, most of them having plenty of problems of their own. Little or no interest was expected from asset strippers, their own assets having fallen in value and the Dunstable site's development potential was also much reduced in the light of the, then, slump in property prices. Moreover, as one cynical journal

Many years before David Brown chose the name All Wheel Drive for the remains of the Bedford truck business, another company with the same name had existed. All Wheel Drive Ltd, of Camberley Surrey, carried out 4x4 and 6x6 conversions to commercial truck chassis until, in 1962, Vickers Armstrongs bought a 60% stake in the Company, renaming it Vickers All Wheel Drive, and moving it to Swindon.

The Company folded in 1971, leaving the name 'vacant' for David Brown to use in the late 'eighties.

noted, the technical press was unlikely to shed tears over a company which had endowed them with so little advertising revenue!

The question arose as to who would be the ideal purchaser. Obviously, the best fit would be with a company which had complementary activities. AWD's strength in exports could, it was felt, attract the attentions of Lonrho, especially as they had recently lost their MAN and VW-Audi concessions. But Lonrho were heavy with debt. The Trinity Group, who had made such a success of Dennis and who were known for buying troubled vehicle producers - like Reliance Mercury and Carmichael - at bargain prices, was another possibility. In the event, one of the companies which once built bodies for war-time Bedfords came to the rescue, in the form of Marshall SPV Limited of Cambridge.

One more chapter in the history of Bedford closed, but another was to open... MILITARY

Largest of all AWD's offerings was to have been the 120-tonne GCW TT 6x6 designed for use as a heavy-duty tractor unit for use with trailers carrying main battle tanks. This had a 14 litre, 400bhp Cummins NTE400 turbo-charged diesel engine and nine-speed range-change Fuller gearbox. Torque was 1150 lbf/ft at 1400rpm. In some people's opinion, a much better-looking rig than the hideous Oshkosh HET which the Army has selected to replace the Scammell Commander. (AWD Limited)

BEDFORD AND MARSHALL SPV

In the 20th part of this series, Robert Coates brings the story almost up-to-date with the acquisition of Bedford-AWD by Marshall Specialist Vehicles

The flat-backed MT 13-18 shown here with the Marshall Matrix ISO-compatible shelter

From its introduction in 1931, right up to the early 'eighties, Bedford lorries enjoyed steady growth and success in military and civilian markets both at home and overseas. In common with most other truck builders, the Company went into decline in the 'eighties as a result of the world-wide slump in sales of commercial vehicles. After much politicking, General Motors effectively abandoned the marque to its fate, dilly-dallying over decisions until it was almost impossible to revive it. AWD made a brave attempt to do so, but their efforts were, ultimately, unsuccessful, having been unable to establish economic levels of production in the depressed world market. After having produced some 15,832 vehicles from the latter half of 1987 to mid-year 1992, they, in turn, had to call in the receivers.

The next chapter in the history of Bedford and their military vehicles started in the autumn of 1992 when Marshall Specialist Vehicles of Cambridge acquired the product design rights - and some of the assets - of AWD Limited. Marshall Specialist Vehicles is part of the Marshall of Cambridge Group, which started business in 1909 providing a chauffeur service to Cambridge University and the surrounding colleges. In 1920, Marshall took on its first vehicle distributorship - with Austin - and in 1929 entered the aviation industry when the company formed a flying school. During WW2, when almost every factory in the land had turned its attention to the war effort, Marshalls were major producers of bodies for Bedford and other makes of military vehicles supplied to the Army. By the 'nineties, the Company had become one of Britain's largest privately-owned firms, with involvement in civil and defence aviation, and road-vehicle work which included the design, building and supply of special purpose vehicles for both the military and civil markets.

Marshalls had acquired the product designs and some of the assets of Carlyle, the Birmingham-based specialist builders of »

A smaller version of DROPS, this MT 26-30 6x6 is seen lifting a 3000-gallon fuel rack which was also produced by Marshall - the brochure points out that 'the equipment can be handled by one man and can collect or deploy the rack within a few minutes'. The TM shown is powered by the 300bhp Perkins Peregrine 8.7-litre turbo-charged and inter-cooled engine.

The ever-popular J-type continued in production with Marshall and still enjoyed quite reasonable overseas sales: it was not available in the UK, although one gained the impression that, with sufficient arm-twisting, any rules could be bent! The Bedford TJ2 11-13 (also known as the TJ2 1100) could be supplied either complete, in stripped-chassis form, or as CKD (completely knocked down) kits. Grossing 11 tonnes, they had naturally-aspirated Perkins Phaser 126bhp engines or Bedford's own diesel which pushed out about 103bhp.

Also available was the slightly heavier TJ2 13-13 which grossed 12 ¹/₂ tonnes and retained the Perkins engine: the old Bedford engine was not available at this weight. In its day, the TJ had been a super vehicle but, even with all Marshall's updates, it had become dated and was decidedly unsuitable for European armies other than, perhaps, as driver-training vehicles.

mini- and midi-buses during 1991/92 and, in the same period, also acquired Essex-based Hoynor, builders of trailers and car transporters. They were still on the acquisition trail when AWD came up for sale. Ultimately, production of all three product lines was transferred to the 475-acre site at the Marshall's-owned Cambridge airport.

A large aircraft hanger at Cambridge was upgraded, with the intention of putting in a new production line to produce a range of Bedford-designed vehicles. Meanwhile, much of the old Bedford site at Dunstable, opposite the deserted Commer-Dodge-Renault works-that-was, was levelled to make way for a new Sainsbury supermarket.

Perhaps this was the first sign of Bedford being about to disappear without trace.

From the onset, Marshall had no intentions of rejoining the volume production rat-race and going into head-on competition with the likes of Iveco-Ford, Leyland-DAF and, probably most significant in their weight ranges at the time, Mercedes-Benz. The way they saw it, there was huge over-capacity in the market up to 17 tonnes, so they planned to concentrate on a smaller Bedford product line-up including TJ 4x2, TL 4x2 and 6x4, and MT 4x4 and 6x6 configurations.

The MT range consisted of derivatives of

the then-current in-service M-type 4x4, and consisted of the MT 15-18 for 15 tonnes gross, and 8 tonnes payload; the MT 17-18 and MT 17-21 - both for 17 tonnes gross, and 10 tonnes payload, but with options of a 180bhp or 210bhp engine; and the MT 19-21, which was for 19 tonnes gross, and 12 tonnes payload. Perkins Phaser engines were used in the export versions, with Cummins in the later Euro-variants.

The MT 26-30 was offered as the new 6x6, offering 'excellent cross-country performance'. Powered by the Perkins Peregrine 8.7 litre turbo-charged and inter-cooled diesel, and using the Fuller nine-speed range-change gearbox, the MT 26-30 was promoted as 'the ideal choice for GS cargo, mobile workshops, tankers, tippers, gritters and a variety of other applications'.

Conspicuous by its absence from their marketing material - even that aimed

specifically at 'Military Logistic Vehicles' - was any reference to the TM, although spares were still available. Presses for the TM body panels were, reportedly, sold to China although, two or three years after Marshalls themselves had 'thrown in the towel', rumour had it that new TM cabs were around, still mounted on their production stillages. AWD's attempts with the (commercial, as distinct from the military) TM

had met with little success and they had failed to revive its fortunes; Marshall simply dropped it from the range.

Marshalls first major export orders were announced in March 1993. Thirty MT 15-18s for Abu Dhabi were sold through the long-term Bedford dealer in the United Arab Emirates, Omeir Bin Youssef & Sons. One of these MTs was the first vehicle to roll off the new Cambridge production line. Another important order was for 70 TJs for Botswana.

In January 1994, Marshalls managed at last to acquire the rights to use the Bedford name in the UK and Europe with 'non-exclusive' rights for the rest of the world. They also purchased the 'Bedford Genuine Parts' organisation, something which, it was hoped, would secure their place much more firmly in the 'after market'. With nearly one

Marshall's production was centred on the MT range, of which these are just two examples. The range was advertised as being suitable for 'ammunition carriers, fuel and water tankers, missile carriers, high-lift platforms, fire tenders, DROPS/PLS, recovery vehicles, shelters, bridge carriers, cargo and box bodies, drill rigs, ISO containers.

Another Marshall's body - just one of some 85,000 units supplied to armies throughout the world since the 'fifties - displayed on an AWD-produced Bedford TM 4-4 8 tonne. The cargo bodies are 'of steel construction with easily detachable support structure and canvas canopies'.

hundred service and parts dealers, world-wide, and with the business reorganised into five divisions, Trucks; Commercial Bodywork; Bus Chassis and Bodywork; Bedford Genuine Parts; and Military Engineering - which designed and made such things as military shelters, ambulance bodywork and logistic vehicle bodies - and with production planned for around 600 trucks a year in 1994, the future looked good.

Over the ensuing years, Marshalls continued to pay attention to export markets, manufacturing and distributing Bedford trucks - albeit in small numbers - to the usual, historic, overseas territories such as Africa and the Middle East. Even their new Marshall-badged 'utility' vehicle (or dustcart!) - a new departure with little, if any, Bedford engineering in it - could be supplied overseas with a Bedford badge if required. Engines continued to be supplied by Perkins and Cummins whilst, for certain overseas markets where it remained popular, the old Bedford diesel engine range could still be obtained in a re-manufactured form, otherwise a Perkins replacement was substituted, dependent on application.

But, by mid-1999, it had all gone pear-shaped again.

Marshall had concentrated their efforts on introducing a stainless-steel bodied midi-bus and an ultra-low entry dustcart rather than the common-or-garden trucks for which Bedford had once been famous. Military sales had been slow to non-existent, especially to the British Army who had invested in Leyland-DAF for their '4 tonnes' and in DROPS for heavier logistics work. In commercial markets, many 'in the trade' felt that Marshall never really picked up the ball and ran with it. There were even rumours - rumours abound in the truck industry! - that Marshall had turned down an order for between 140 and 400 TMs.

Certainly the Company was not to be seen at any of the shows which Bedford had at one time frequented.

In the event, they sold out their Bedford Genuine Parts business to ERF along with the rights to the 'Class 8' utility cab and midi-bus chassis for £5.25 million. ERF intended to integrate this business with their own parts business and those of Western Star of Canada, the then-owners of ERF. Marshall was to continue with their traditional work including the supply of 'transport-related' products - like vehicle-mounted NBC ('nuclear, biological and chemical') shelters and so forth.

ERF has now changed hands and is owned by MAN of Germany, in which there was a faint irony - at least insofar as the military vehicles are concerned, MAN having supplied lorries to the German Army, against which so many Bedfords had fought.

What was thought to be probably the last chapter in the history of the classic military vehicle opened with the 'scuttle' going round the truck business suggesting that Bedford parts were 'difficult to obtain' and that the new Company was 'not really supporting the distributors'.

Against that, however, some 600 TMs were alleged to be 'up for' refurbishment and it was felt that there must be someone who would be interested in providing a service to the 16,000 Bedfords still operating in the UK, (including about 9000 in the Ministry of Defence) to say nothing of the 160,000-plus reported to be going strong, world-wide.

...and there was!

In August 2002, Amethyst Group Logistics Division was appointed to run the Bedford Genuine Parts (BGP) business and all the indications are that they intend to make a go of it. In what is described in their press release as 'a parallel move' Automotive Group Limited (AGL), formerly known to many as Autoflow, and the ultimate parent of Amethyst, acquired the design and marketing rights to BGP from ERF. Managing Director Phil King tells me that the business will be highly computerised, which will enable them to provide a cost-effective service to end-users. Good luck to them: it would be a pity, now that truck production is well and truly dead and buried, to see the Bedford name disappear altogether.

The 'oldies' will continue to be looked after by our old friend 'Bygone Bedford Bits' and it is comforting to know, now, that the not-so-oldies can also be taken care of. █

This Bedford MT 26-30 would have been quite an impressive rig if it had ever seen service. With a payload capacity of 16 tonnes and a gross train weight of 32 tonnes, the MT6x6 was seen as an 'ideal'(!) solution for rapid re-supply operations.

All photographs courtesy of Marshall SPV Limited

BEDFORD ENGINES

Robert Coates takes a look at the various engines which were used to power Bedford's military vehicles over the years

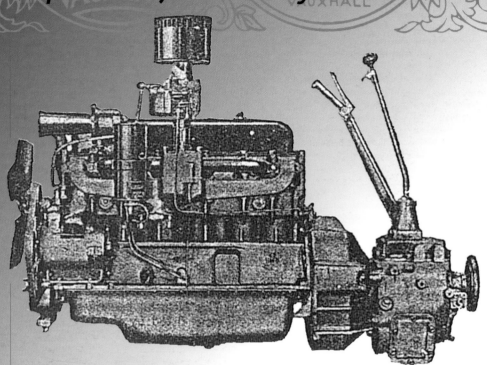

Left: The 27HP or '194in³ petrol' engine, used in all models from 1931 to July 1938. In his book, published in 1961, F A Stepney Acres, Bedford's Chief Engineer was of the opinion that few of these now survived.

However, it would have featured in some of the Bedfords which were impressed or requisitioned for the War effort in September 1939.

215in³ PETROL ENGINE

Good as the '27HP' engine was, Bedford engineers were eager to improve it - a feature which kept them at the forefront of British truck production for over 50 years. Modifications were made to reduce fuel consumption and the new engine, the 'improved 28HP', came on-stream in July 1938, in time to be fitted to the new K, M and O Types and all Bedford's war-time vehicles. It remained in continuous production, virtually unchanged, to March 1951.

Bore and stroke were enlarged, to 3³/₈in and 4in, respectively, and the compression ratio was increased to 6.22:1 which put maximum power output up to 72bhp at a slightly-higher - ungoverned - 3000rpm. Torque was also improved, to 161 lbf/ft at the same revs as the older engine. The 27.34HP RAC output was rounded-up to 28HP.

The new unit featured a counter-balanced, four-bearing crankshaft, a new shape combustion chamber with a 'controlled flame' system, plus various

O ne only has to look down a list of rally entrants or, indeed, the 'runners' on such events as the HCVS London to Brighton Run to see that there is often confusion about which engine is installed in which Bedford. But engine options were not available from Bedford until after the War, so what's the problem?

Some of the confusion is caused by the fact that Bedford had no engine-type identification of their own. In the pre-war period they were known by their RAC 'horsepower' rating. Post-war, the engines were described by cubic capacity and, in some cases, fuel system, and Bedford, probably uniquely in the British market, described engine capacities in cubic inches. Thus a typical post-war engine might be described as '194in³ petrol' or '300in³ diesel'.

Where there were differences in detail between engines of the same displacement used in different chassis, the engine number carried a prefix relating to its intended chassis type: for example, military post-war, re-conditioned engines carried the suffix 'R'. But sometimes there were no clues and any differences were 'just something you were expected to know'! On the war-time 3-tonners, for example, there were subtle differences between the engines fitted to OYs and QLs - one such being different inlet arrangements to the water pump.

Below, I have described each of Bedford's engines, in the order they were introduced.

194in³ PETROL ENGINE

Bedford's first engine was a six-cylinder, in-line, overhead-valve, side-cam, petrol unit of 3179cc which was known by Bedford as the 194in³ model, but described by everybody else as the '27HP'. Bore and

stroke dimensions were 3⁵/₁₆in x 3³/₄in, giving an RAC rating of 26.3HP, rounded up to 27. With a compression ratio of 5.6:1, the power output was 64bhp at 2800rpm, and torque was 142 lbf/ft at 1200rpm.

This engine was factory fitted to all models to July 1938 but the '27HP' is very unlikely to feature in any military vehicles - except perhaps an early prototype of the MW.

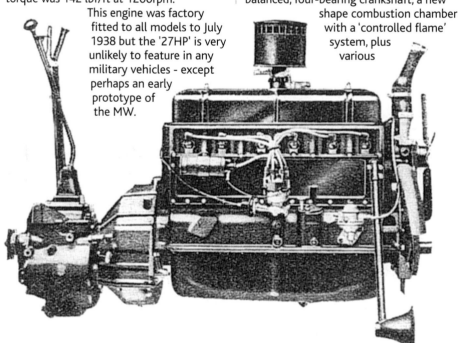

The 28HP engine, also known as the '215in³ petrol', used from July 1938 in all models, including all military production, until March 1951. Hailed by 'Commercial Motor' magazine as having 'high output, economy and durability'. Note the air scoop at the foot of the ventilation tube on this early version. Some 400,000 of these engines were built.

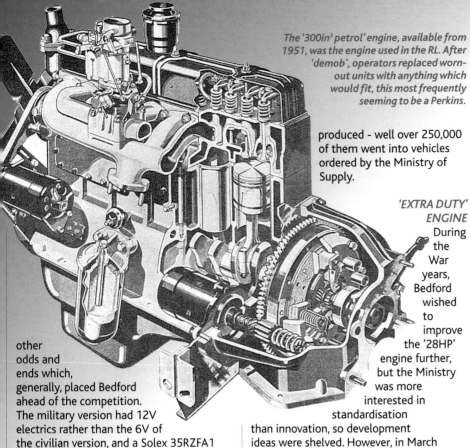

The '300in³ petrol' engine, available from 1951, was the engine used in the RL. After 'demob', operators replaced worn-out units with anything which would fit, this most frequently seeming to be a Perkins.

The 'Extra Duty' engine, of which there were two versions, was introduced in March 1951. The two versions differed in their carburettor size and jet settings, which affected the ultimate power output. The less-powerful version, which would be unlikely to be found in any military vehicle, was discontinued with the A range, whilst the more powerful one - which could have found its way, as a replacement into OX, OY or OW models - carried on until 1958.

other odds and ends which, generally, placed Bedford ahead of the competition. The military version had 12V electrics rather than the 6V of the civilian version, and a Solex 35RZFA1 carburettor in place of a down-draught Zenith.

Improvements to the 'improved' engine met three design objectives - economy, performance and longevity. Although the old engine was quite economical, the new unit ran at a lower speed; the civilian M Type 2-tonner, basis of the MW, ran at 1480rpm at 30mph, compared with its previous 1655rpm, and for the O Type 3-tonner (basis of the OX and OY), revs dropped from 2100rpm to 1830.

Running at a lower speed consumed less fuel, and also improved durability. More power also produced more torque at the rear wheels, benefiting acceleration and speed. Fuel consumption was estimated to be 5-15% better than the old engine - a major improvement.

About 400,000 of these engines were

produced - well over 250,000 of them went into vehicles ordered by the Ministry of Supply.

'EXTRA DUTY' ENGINE
During the War years, Bedford wished to improve the '28HP' engine further, but the Ministry was more interested in standardisation than innovation, so development ideas were shelved. However, in March 1951, an 'Extra Duty' version of the 28HP was made available. This was used in K, M and O models from this date onwards so any WW2 vehicles fitted with the 'Extra Duty' engine have had it fitted as a replacement.

The engine used the same dimensions, and differed little from the standard version, but incorporated improvements to increase its useful working life. There were two versions of this unit, differing only in their carburettor specification which, of course, influenced power output - the K and M models had a 76bhp unit, the O Types produced 84bhp.

In early 1957, came an even more improved version of the 'Extra Duty' engine. Still at 214.7in³ (3519cc), but with

Out with the old, in with the new: an MJ undergoing a change of heart with a new Bedford '330in³ turbo-diesel' engine. The photo was taken in the workshops of the Royal Marines Logistic Regiment near Barnstaple, in Devon to whom many thanks for their active co-operation.

compression ratio pushed up to 6.75:1 and power up to 100bhp. This was the engine for the newly-announced C and D Types.

The old RAC rating system had been discontinued by this time as taxation was no longer calculated by this method, so we just have the capacity or the bhp to go by unless, as in this case, the engine actually had a name. The 'Extra Duty' was a higher-revving engine, achieving its power at 3600rpm, although it was usually governed to 3500. None of these engines was used in military vehicles - at least as OEM ('original equipment manufacture') - but they may have found their way into ex-WW2 vehicles as replacements.

300in³ PETROL ENGINE
Introduced in 1951, this was the engine which powered the RL military range, the S Type and some of the larger C and D Type

civilian vehicles. Bedford retained the six-cylinder, in-line, engine format with a bore of 3⁷/₈in and a stroke of 4¹/₄in, giving 300.75in³ capacity, or about 4.9 litres.

It was an engine which kept on being improved. The earliest versions, to January 1957, had a compression ratio of 6:1, but this was increased to 6.5:1 for engines up to number 3621 for the R Type; the very latest models had a 6.6:1 ratio. This affected power output, of course, with the three phases having 110bhp at 3200 rpm, 115bhp at 3000 rpm, and 133bhp at 3400 rpm, respectively. Torque was 234 lbf/ft at 1200 rpm, 240 at 1400, and 267 at 1200.

The '300' was a nice, smooth engine to drive and retained the classic Bedford sound, which is more than can be said for the next Bedford engine to be announced. Also a 300in³ unit, but one with a difference.

300in³ DIESEL ENGINE

This engine was introduced in 1957 simultaneously with the launch of the civilian C and D truck ranges, and as the diesel option on the S Type - but not the RL - to counter competition from both Perkins and Leyland.

Bore and stroke details were the same as the 300 petrol engine, but the block and various other components were strengthened to take the stresses imposed by a diesel. Interestingly, these features were then adopted as the standard for the 300in³ petrol engine which thus became a very robust unit.

The diesel's power output was dramatically different from the petrol version. The 'knocker' could only manage a measly, and noisy, 97bhp at 2800rpm with a compression ratio of 17:1. Unusually, it was governed to 3000rpm - above its theoretical maximum power output! Torque was almost equally depressing, 217 lbf/ft at 1400rpm.

A smaller, four-cylinder version of this engine was produced for use at the small end of the TJ range and this one had to be heard to be believed! It need not concern us here.

'60' AND '70' SERIES ENGINES

In 1966, Bedford announced two new engines: the 60 and 70 series. These were of 381in³ and 466in³ capacity respectively but, as they were not used in military vehicles, these, too, can be passed over.

330 ENGINE

This was the engine fitted in MK military vehicles. It had a bore of 4¹/₁₆in whilst retaining the stroke measurement of its predecessor, the 300, making it the nearest to a 'square' engine that Bedford ever produced. The version used in the MK was a multi-fuel unit, capable of running on petrol, diesel or various types of aviation fuels - similar to DERV. It would, so the story goes, even run on melted peanut butter but any records of this actually happening must have been mislaid somewhere.

Its 330in³ - 5.49 litres - produced 105bhp at 2800rpm and it continued in use until the introduction of the MJ, which was basically the same vehicle - plus a few little cosmetic updates - with a turbo-charged, but non-multi-fuel, 330 engine.

Both of these engines are still fairly easy to come by, the latter being easily identifiable by the the turbocharger.

500 in³ ENGINE

The military TM, introduced in 1978, had Bedford's 500 engine, the last produced by Bedford. It was an 8198cc in-line, direct injection four-stroke whose design was based on the '70' series unit. Bedford's designers must have reached the limit on how much they could increase the bore so, instead, lengthened the stroke. This, of course, meant a total 'bottom end' redesign, including a new crankshaft. Power output was 151bhp at only 2500rpm compared with the 466's 2800rpm.

It may be a while before these start appearing on the rally field so, perhaps, any more detail at this stage is superfluous.

A22 'CHURCHILL' ENGINE

This is unlikely to be confused with any of the engines appearing in Bedford's main-line military vehicle, but whilst on the subject of engines, it would be a pity to omit it!

The Bedford-designed Churchill tank engine was a 21-litre side-valve job which was created, from scratch, in less than 90 days. This feat resulted in Bedford being given responsibility for Churchill tank

The Bedford '500in³ engine' as used in the TM 4-4 8 tonne and the TM 6-6 14 tonne. When driving the TM, the temptation is to keep one's foot down simply to hear the song of this lovely engine's turbo-charger! Again, thanks to the Royal Marines for access to their workshops to take this photograph (and have a general 'snoop round'!)

The '500in³ turbo-diesel' was an 8.2 litre unit being an uprated version of the 60 and 70 series diesels used in commercial chassis of which this cutaway drawing is an illustration. The '60' unit had a capacity of 381in³ (6.2 litres) and the '70', 466in³ (7.6 litres).

production. Developing 350bhp from its flat-12 arrangement of cylinders, it no longer had the classic Bedford sound but, with one and three-quarter litres per 'pot', was a delight to hear. ■

BEDFORD 'HEAVY VEHICLE A22'

Robert Coates describes the Churchill heavy infantry tank

'**H**eavy vehicle, A22' was the War Office style nomenclature adopted by Vauxhall Motors, Bedford's parent Company, for what became the Churchill tank. The Company was rightly proud of their achievement with the Churchill, stating 'Luton's most spectacular war product was, without doubt, the Churchill tank. In 1940 with invasion apparently imminent, the British Army had fewer than 100 tanks available in this country. Vauxhall was asked to design and build a new tank. Normally production of a new tank from original drawings to finished product took about four years. Starting virtually from scratch, Vauxhall had the 38-ton Churchill tank coming off the line in one year. Ten other factories had to be parented to assemble the Churchill from Luton-made parts. By War's end, 5640 Churchill tanks had been built and just over 3000 of these were rebuilt after damage in action. It was an incredible achievement.'

Those are the bare facts, but there was rather more to it than that. Vauxhall/Bedford's experience of designing and building tanks had, up to the time they were commissioned to design the A22, been confined to 'lending a hand' to the Mechanisation Board on such things as cooling systems and suspension. Their first 'proper' engagement was to design a 350bhp petrol engine for the A20.

Hitherto, Bedford had only produced engines of 27 and 28 RAC horsepower, but this one would have had an RAC rating of 120 horsepower. Bedford engines had always had overhead valves, but their first attempt at a 350bhp engine simply would not fit in the space provided so they had to revert to side valves. Wooden mock-ups were built, to check for accessibility for routine maintenance - which had to be carried out from the top - and to see that it would be possible to assemble on a production line. In the event, they came up with a working product in under 90 days... only to find that the A20 had been abandoned.

It had been decided to go back to the drawing board and start again with a brand-new design for an infantry tank. The A20 specification dated from 1938-39 and described a slow - 10mph - machine with frontal armour that was two feet thick, probably more appropriate to the Great War than to WW2. By mid-1940, Harland & Wolff, of Belfast, had built a running mild-steel prototype, but it was unsatisfactory in several respects - especially in the engine and gearbox departments.

It was undoubtedly Bedford's remarkably quick turn-round on the engine that landed them the job of designing and producing the new A22 - a tank that was to be of a weight and size not previously experienced anywhere. It must be said that the Company had lots of help from 'outside' including that of Dr H E Merritt, Director of Tank Design, who actually moved to Luton to be on hand for the project.

Work started in July 1940 and continued over weekends and Bank Holidays - not unusual in British industry in those dire times. There was no time for proper prototyping; if it worked, it went into production and improvements were carried out as experience was gained. Some testing, particularly of the engine and tracks, was carried out in the obsolete A20 hull.

In their little post-war booklet, 'An account of our stewardship', Vauxhall noted that their first record runs were of 30-40 miles. Gradually these records were beaten, with 'runs of 100 miles, 500 miles, 1000 miles' and, by June 1941, the first batch of 14 had been completed. The problems were, eventually, overcome although there were, for some time - probably right up to the Churchill III version - worries about reliability. General Brooke, later Field Marshall Lord Alanbrooke, Chief of the Imperial General Staff and Churchill's right-hand man, notes in his diary for 10 May 1941 that he '... went on with Martel to Luton to see the new heavy tank... the A22, which is now nearing completion. Had a drive round

The first Churchill, the infantry tank Mk IV, carried a 3in howitzer in the driving compartment with a 2-pounder quick-firing gun and a 7.92mm Besa co-axial machine gun in a single-piece cast turret. The Churchill II, or infantry tank Mk IVA, was almost identical but, in place of the howitzer, there was another 7.92mm Besa.

On the production line, each chassis was connected by chains to the next in line; as one tank was finished, it was started up and driven off the production line, pulling all the others along with it.

Churchill Ark 'ramp tank' which carried another tank on its back to allow obstacles to be crossed - this is of the so-called 'Italian pattern' with no trackway over the hull. (Tank Museum)

Early prototype with a small wooden mock-up turret.

Churchill mine clearance tank. (Tank Museum)

Churchill bridgelayer. (IWM, KID 3133)

The Churchill III had a welded turret but in other respects was similar to the Churchill IV (shown), which reverted to a single-piece casting. Armament was identical. The Churchill V retained the one-piece turret and the two Besa machine guns, but the 6-pounder main armament was replaced by a 95mm howitzer.

and took over the steering from the dual-controlled seat of the howitzer gunner. Then visited factory to see tanks constructed on a motor-car principle. The tank promises extraordinarily well. I wish we had a hundred of them.'

Vauxhall/Bedford did not have the factory capacity to carry out all the work themselves and much had to be contracted out, both on the manufacture and assembly side. New test buildings and rigs had to be set up and new dynamometers obtained - not an easy task in war-time. The Ministry of Supply also stipulated that, as far as possible, capacity should be employed which was not already engaged on war work, which was an almost impossible demand. Ten major contractors were engaged in production, in addition to the scores of tiny workshops all over the country, some of which were capable of carrying out only one process, before passing on to another 'dispersed' workshop for the next process. The terrifying inefficiency of such a scheme could really only be contemplated in war-time, when backs were against the wall and there was no alternative. The transport costs alone would make it economically non-viable in peace-time.

To improve efficiency on the final assembly line, an ingenious device was employed by Vauxhall. No moving production line was available, certainly not one which could cope with the weight involved, and no time or materials existed to build one. To overcome

The Churchill VII incorporated a lot of changes. Armour plating was thicker and formed part of the hull (earlier versions had the armour bolted on). The turret was of composite cast and plate design, and was thicker. Armament remained unchanged from the VI version. The final 'edition' of the Churchill (shown) was similar to the VII in every way, except that the armament was, once more, a 95 mm howitzer.

this, each chassis was connected by chains to the next in line. As one tank was finished, it was started up and driven off the production line, pulling all the others along with it and creating a space at the back of the line for the next to be laid down. Not a bad test for a brand-new engine and vehicle!

Between them, Vauxhall/Bedford and their associates built 5640 Churchills of which about 2000 were Churchill Is and IIs (infantry tanks, Mk IV and Mk IVA). Many were converted into 'specials' including the AVRE - 'armoured vehicle, Royal Engineers' - with its stubby, howitzer-like device which hurled a charge about the size of a dustbin at pillboxes and other concrete obstructions. Others included the famous Crab 'flail' for exploding

mines, the 'Crocodile' trailer-towing flame-thrower, the wooden-bundle-carrying 'fascine', various types of portable bridge, and armoured recovery vehicles (ARVs) and beach ARVs.

Dimensions of the 40-ton Churchill had to be set within limits which would allow movement by rail, as this was the conventional way of bringing armour nearer to the front line. In the event, the Churchill, which was 302 inches long, 128 inches wide and 98 inches high, was right on the limit for rail transport and required very careful 'centering' on the war-time railway flat cars.

Suspension was of a new type for British tanks, consisting of 11 road wheels each side, independently mounted on short trailing arms and sprung on vertical springs.

The most fascinating aspect of the design was the engine. Contrary to what some reference books would have you believe, it was not simply two Bedford truck engines 'bolted together': two times 72bhp does not give you 350bhp!

A first for the Luton designers, and 'a bit

Churchill Crocodile VII flame-thrower tank - the Crocodile towed a pressurised trailer containing inflammable liquid which was discharged through a nozzle in the bow of the tank.

Engine specification

CONSTRUCTION DETAILS: 12-cylinder (twin-six), horizontally-opposed; seven-bearing, counter-balanced crankshaft; alloy pistons running in short cylinder liners; 'L'-shaped combustion chambers with two spark plugs per cylinder; sodium-cooled exhaust valves with Stellite valve-seat inserts; hardened crankshaft journals; dry-sump lubrication with de-aerating and oil-cooling systems; finned-tube oil coolers combined with radiators at the rear on each side.

PERFORMANCE DATA: capacity, $1296in^3$ (21,238cc); bore/stroke, 5in x $5^1/_2$in, giving 120 RAC horsepower; power output, 350bhp at 2200rpm; torque, 960 lbf/ft at 800-1600rpm.

CARBURETTORS: four 46 mm Solex 46FNHE; consumption, 0.57 lb/bhp per hour.

Churchill AVRE ('armoured vehicle Royal Engineers') equipped with concrete wrecking ball and Petard spigot mortar for demolition work.

unusual' by any standards, was the cylinder configuration - it was essentially, a twelve cylinder 'twin-six' horizontally-opposed unit of $1296in^3$ (21,238cc) capacity which, in spite of its size, was 'dreadfully under-powered' for the task it had to perform. With a 5in bore and a stroke of $5^1/_2$in, it was, in the Bedford tradition, a 'long-stroke' engine developing a nominal 350bhp at 2200rpm. Fuel consumption was stated as being 0.57 lb/bhp per hour which, according to my calculations and assumptions about speed at full power, represents something on the wrong side of one mile per gallon!

Whilst the long stroke was very much in the Bedford tradition, the side valves were certainly not, but how much better, or more powerful, the engine might have been with overhead valves will remain a matter for conjecture. Special features were incorporated to improve durability. Yet, in spite of these, and in spite of the continuous programme of improvements, the dear old Churchill was not very durable, or reliable, or fast, or heavily armed... all of which made the Prime Minister,

Mr Churchill, 'not too happy' about the tank having taken his name.

The first examples were equipped with a pitiful 2-pounder anti-tank gun, which one critic described as being like a peashooter on an elephant. The gun was all that was available and it cannot be denied that it was, at least, a tank, and tanks were what the Army was short of.

The Churchill first saw active service in the 1942 Dieppe raid, at which so much was learned in preparation for D-Day. It did stalwart service in North Africa and, together with its many derivatives, in the battles of north-west Europe. On retirement, many of its special roles were taken over by its successor, the Centurion. However, at Tankfest 2002, one was to be seen trundling majestically round the arena - an inspiring sight. MILITARY

Experiments with a turret-less Churchill ARV ('armoured recovery vehicle') towing a tracked trailer - production Churchill ARVs were fitted with a dummy turret and gun. (Tank Museum).

GREEN GODDESS

Robert Coates takes a detailed look at what must be one of the longest-serving 'green machines' in the Western world - the Bedford RLHZ, or Green Goddess

The Bedford self-propelled heavy pump unit, RLHZ, better known by its nickname, the Green Goddess, is not, strictly, a military vehicle being 'owned', maintained and operated by the Office of the Deputy Prime Minister. However, it is indisputably a 'green machine' and, since the early-fifties, Goddesses have provided emergency back-up to the fire services around the UK. They have appeared from time to time on the television news - during various firemen's strikes, or relieving the effects of flooding - such as at Chichester in West Sussex when, over the course of a couple of weeks, they pumped away millions of gallons of floodwater, or again at a huge moorland fire in South Yorkshire a few years back. More recently, they have been in the news with the national firemen's strike which started in November 2002 and has only recently been resolved.

Originally intended for civil-defence work, there remain some 800 or so vehicles in service, held in store at Marchington, in Staffordshire 'against any eventuality'; 52 vehicles are usually kept on immediate stand-by, ready to turn the key and drive away, with their 'first-aid' tanks charged with up to 400 gallons of water. The remainder of the fleet can be made ready in next to no time as they are 'exercised' periodically on a journey of 10-15 miles on local roads. They must at all times be road-worthy and task-worthy - ie, they must be able to earn their living by being able to pump! Often, their drivers are much younger than the vehicles themselves - many have never even seen a Goddess before and hardly any have had to engage in the old-fashioned process of double de-clutching

Technically, there is not a lot to say about the RLHZ - it is, more or less, a standard RL fitted with a special body and a lot of extra equipment - early versions were based on the Bedford SHZ 'special appliance' 4x2 chassis. The RLHS was chosen because it was 'simple to drive and operate and required the

A privately-owned, and very smart, Green Goddess. This example - number 7614 - was issued to Teeside Airport before passing into private hands.

The new EFS (Emergency Fire Service) logo which was to replace the original AFS - Auxiliary Fire Service.

'By the right . . . dress! It is hard to believe the age of these immaculately lined-up vehicles in their temperature- and humidity-controlled store: they seem, in every sense, to be as good as new. Tyres are kept inflated to 100 lbf/in^2 to ensure that flat-spots do not develop during their lengthy standing periods.

minimum of skilled maintenance'. Papworth Industries built the special bodywork, which contains a comprehensive range of fire-fighting accessories including hose reels in the centre lockers on both sides - there is even a stirrup pump with chimney attachment which is still, apparently, the most effective way of dealing with chimney fires! The main pump, a Sigmund FN4 fed from a 300 or 400 gallon tank, has an output of 900gal/min at 100 lbf/in^2, and can be used to provide four good fire-fighting jets or used as a relay pump with 6in diameter hoses.

Due to their age, the Goddesses are exempt from normal plating and testing, yet they are maintained and tested to the same standards as would be required if they were not. Equipment on the vehicles is also maintained to the same high standards with, for example, delivery hoses being pneumatically-tested periodically, following which they are dried and 'chalked' (with French chalk) to prevent the insides from sticking together.

The Goddesses were originally owned, operated and maintained by the Home Office, and were stored around the UK in five locations. A few years ago the maintenance

component was put out to contract and one of the reasons TNT Truckcare won the initial contract was their recommendation to concentrate everything in four storage buildings at Marchington in Staffordshire. Three of the four buildings hold Goddesses, the fourth holds stocks of general spares.

The spares stock seems vast. It took four years to concentrate everything at Marchington, involving a massive inspection and stock-taking exercise and recording the whole lot on computer. There is a small element of secondhand and refurbished spares, including radiators, fuel tanks, crankshafts, generators, lamps, CCFW (Coventry-Climax Feather Weight) pump trolleys and so on. There is also a large stock of new parts - including new crankshafts, still in their crates. Many of the faster moving spares - like filters and fan belts - can still be bought off the shelf, so it tends to be the slower moving, more 'out-of-the-way', spares which make up the refurbished item count. Spares cover is reckoned to be 'adequate for the foreseeable future'.

An interesting situation arose with brake cylinders, some of which showed signs of rust from water absorbed into the brake

fluid. Honing the rusty area resulted in an imperfect fit for the seals and oversize kits were not available. The solution was to bore out the old cylinders, re-sleeve them and use the original seal kits.

The stock of tyres, serviced annually for pressure and condition, is huge and there are many different tread patterns and makes, including Avon, Goodyear and Barnum, but they are never mixed on any one vehicle. In reserve stock, the tyres are kept inflated at normal pressures (fitted to wheels, of course). On the vehicles, pressures are increased to prevent flat-spots developing. Another good idea for old vehicle owners for the winter months - only don't forget to set the right pressures before the first outing of the season!

Good as the Goddesses are, they are now over 50 years old and, some years back, various problems were foreseen. Amongst these was the fact that four-star petrol was to disappear in December 1999. Second, at 7-8mpg, they were hardly economical, a factor which came into play as they were often used miles from hard standing - let alone a petrol station. Third, although with a following wind on the flat, they could attain 45-50mph, they were slow. And fourth, spares were becoming more difficult to obtain.

At the time, care of the fleet was contracted to TNT's Truckcare division, and it was hoped to persuade the Home Office, under whose responsibility they fell, to allow them to be up-graded. This was seen as being 'a whole lot greener' than buying new ones; it would certainly have worked out a whole lot cheaper!

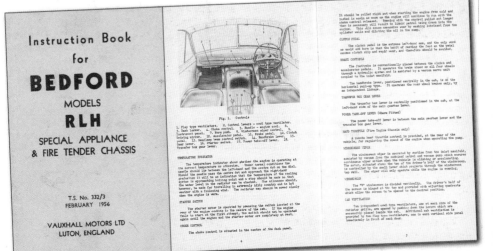

Third edition of the instruction book for the RLHC and RLHZ - dated February 1956; the first edition was published in August 1953.

Filling first-aid water tanks prior to issue from the Marchington depot. The tanks hold 300 gallons of water although earlier models - which were based on the Bedford SHZ chassis (4x2 for special appliances) had 400 gallon tanks mounted further back so that the hose-reels had to be fitted into the rear lockers.

Sales brochure dating from 1960 for the 'commercial' Bedford R Type truck and chassis showing the RLHZ - chassis and cowl variant.

To ensure that they are not mistaken for military vehicles, Green Goddesses deployed in Northern Ireland are painted yellow. They are, otherwise, of the same specification as the standard green version. A general-purpose lorry is also retained in the same colours.

The main thrust of the proposed upgrade was the fitting of a diesel engine. Diesels are safer than petrol, especially for fire appliances, but more importantly, at the time the fuel was cheaper than 4-star petrol and would have improved the consumption figure of the Goddess to about 14mpg. The search began for a suitable unit even though the Home Office made no commitment to the project whatsoever - not even guaranteeing funding if the project was successful.

Various engines were considered and rejected for one reason or another - nobody wanted 'a great big engine which could give 100mph' and, ultimately, the Cummins B Series, four-cylinder unit was chosen. There was, though, at least one other contender, a well-known Bedford dealer, who experimented - unsuccessfully, as it turned out - with fitting a Perkins unit. The Cummins unit developed 112bhp (not that much different from the old Bedford's 110bhp). What would have happened to all the old Bedford petrol engines if the re-fit had gone ahead was a matter for conjecture, especially as most of them were still like new; they would certainly have been worth getting one's hands on.

A five- or six-speed gearbox was also proposed and, again, several options were evaluated, including automatic. Cummins and ZF took on the problem of working out the gradability, speeds through the gears, etc, and it transpired that the B Series engine's power curve, coupled with a ZF five-speed 'box was well suited to the power take-off requirements of the pump which needs 1500rpm to do its work properly.

Amongst other upgrades considered and rejected was power-assisted steering. The original RLs have no power assistance and the tapered chassis is not really suitable for retrofitting it, quite apart from the unsuitability of the large steering wheel. A cab-

heater was given the go-ahead as it was felt to be necessary for firemen who have been working in cold weather. Also, the vehicle was to be completely rewired not only to meet the needs of a diesel vehicle, but also because of the electrical upgrade required by improved on-board equipment.

The entire re-furb job was to consist of a whole list of things including fitting new beacons, sidelights, scene lights and new flashing lights - blue at the front linked with the headlamps, red/blue alternate at rear. Additionally, a 'white noise', urban, directional siren was to have been fitted - you cannot 'focus' on the direction of a two-tone. Also a PA system; roller shutter locker doors - the originals are prone to jamming shut; electrically-heated mirrors; upgraded vacuum system (the present braking system runs directly off the manifold - the proposed one was to have had a reserve vacuum tank). New gauges were to be fitted, especially on the prototype, on which everything would have been monitored. Finally, the machine was to be repainted in a brighter, almost 'day-glow' green with a red-and-white stripe. A local university advised on the design which disguises the 'old' bulbous nose shape. A new logo (EFS, Emergency Fire Service, not AFS) was actually painted on to a trial vehicle.

One way or another, this amounted to a very significant upgrade!

Suppliers were, of course, very helpful: this would have been good business in its own right - as well as wonderful publicity. It perhaps seems astonishing that all this work was seen as worth doing on a vehicle of this

relative antiquity, but Truckcare contended that the Goddesses still had much to offer - in some respects more than the modern 'red' fire engines. For example, four-wheel drive, high ground clearance, huge pumping capacity, and the ability to act as a water relay pump for really major jobs. And they are in such astonishingly good condition, looking perfectly business-like... even if a little dated; mileages are minute when their age is taken into consideration, and even the chequer-plate on most of the vehicles is still factory sharp.

Unfortunately, the upgrade which was carried out amounted simply to conversion of some, possibly all, of the existing engines to use unleaded fuel. As to which of the remaining wish-list was actually implemented, it has not been possible to ascertain. Similarly, surviving vehicle numbers and other information is scant - a letter, headed 'Office of the Deputy Prime Minister' and subtitled 'Emergency Fire Service' informs me that 'vehicle numbers and operational needs' will be assessed once the firemen's dispute is resolved, so maybe we shall soon be able to obtain an update.

It is worth pointing out that other versions of the RL were also adopted by the Civil Defence authorities - one such frequently seen on the rally-field, is the RL hoselayer but this is not a 'Green Goddess', the name being reserved for the 'heavy pump unit' only...

... and these lovely old machines soldier on doing the job they were built for over 50 years ago. **MILITARY**

BEDFORD ROUND-UP · 1

Robert Coates starts to wind up the Bedford series by looking at the Company's output up to 1945.

Despite its chunky appearance, the 'BT' Bedford tractor, or Traclat as it was known - short form for 'TRACked Light Artillery Tractor' - was only 252x90in, with a height of 108in, scarcely larger than a standard GS lorry… but it must have been a lot more fun to drive. (IWM, MVE 9554/6, 9554/7)

Up to the outbreak of WW2, Bedford produced two major ranges of lorry. The W Type two-tonner, dating from 1931, was upgraded to three tons in 1934 and was much improved, being renamed WT. In 1938, a complete new range was introduced: the K Type for 10/12cwt; the 30cwt M Type, and the O Type, the latter eventually taking the range up to five tons. This range stayed in production until 1952 having, in the meantime, spawned the 'sub-range' of war-time vehicles - the MW 15cwt, based on the M Type; the 'O' range, consisting of the OW and OWB utility civilian models; and the OX and OY military models.

The MW was, effectively, a 'War Office' M Type and it seems likely that the OW was Bedford's initial offering as a three-tonner for military use. In the event, the OW did not go into production until September 1941, and then only for civilians. Further modifications to the civilian O Type, to meet military requirements, resulted in the OX (short wheelbase) and OY (long wheelbase) designations. There was also the QL 4x4 3-tonner which was almost a range in its own right, and was described in some detail in the April to September 2002 issues. Other, major, war-time vehicle production included the Churchill tank, or 'heavy vehicle A22', described in the August 2003 issue.

During the War, Bedford produced more than 250,000 lorries for the armed forces -

equivalent to about 1000 a week for five years. In the unlikely event that this lot could have ended up parked nose to tail, the queue would have extended further than from Land's End to John O' Groats. Bedford also provided all the spare parts that this huge fleet required, amounting to some £18.5 million at the time, and equivalent to £500-600 million at today's prices.

In addition to the vehicles and spares, Bedford - or more strictly, Vauxhall Motors - produced a plethora of other war-like material. Four million venturi tubes were

manufactured for rocket projectiles, plus jigs, tools, and fixtures. Dies were produced for the Hercules engine, for the duration of the War. And, on one occasion, when 'tin hats' were scarce and needed in a hurry, Vauxhall produced 750,000 of them. Aircraft development work was carried out on the Mosquito twin-engined fighter bomber, and the Halifax and Lancaster medium and heavy bombers. In great secrecy, Vauxhall also worked

79

The 3-ton 4x2 OY was another specialised military type, seen here in OYC configuration with a water tanker body - note the detachable hoops which were intended to support a canvas cover, disguising the vehicle as a standard cargo truck. (Vauxhall Motors)

...and, in their spare time, Vauxhall also produced mines, shells, torpedoes, radio-location devices, bombs, tin hats, and jerrycans.

The 4x4 QL was Bedford's contribution to the 3-ton class. 52,245 QLs were produced from February 1941 - most were equipped, as these, with GS cargo bodies but there were also troop-carrying, tractor, tanker, fire appliance, radio, office, and tipper variants.

Although Bedford also continued to produce civilian vehicles during the War, albeit in restricted numbers and only for authorised users, many ex-military vehicles were snapped up by commercial operators when large-scale disposals started. This is almost certainly an ex-military 6-ton OXC tractor, photographed in Crouch End, North London in service with the Post Office Supplies Department.

on the first 12 aircraft jet engines.

Throughout the early part of the War, up to the end of the North African campaign, petrol was distributed in 'flimsies' - tin cans which held about two gallons and which were very prone to leakage. These were needed in vast numbers and at least one 'tin-can' factory was set up in Egypt to allow petrol to be shipped in bulk and 'canned' locally. When the first 'jerrycan' was captured, it was rushed to Luton for copying. Vauxhall eventually pressed 5,000,000 jerrycan sides, and these were welded-up at small plants dispersed around the country. A couple of years ago, there was a 'scare' that Britain might be sued for breach of patent for copying the design but, fortunately, it came to nothing.

In the field of armaments, Vauxhall-Bedford produced mines, torpedoes, radio-location devices - the fore-runner of radar - bombs and, during one emergency period, 6-pounder armour-piercing shot at the rate of 6000 rounds per week. They were also closely involved with experiments in waterproofing vehicles (see panel). Even the styling department was involved, becoming expert in camouflage, designing decoy trucks and aircraft, aircraft 'hides' and a host of other bits and pieces.

Bedford was also heavily involved with development work. Their aircraft-related projects have already been mentioned and, in

previous articles, their work on the Churchill tank, the 'wading giraffe', the Bedford Bren and so on. At one stage in the War, Bedford was supplied with some captured German half- and three-quarter tracked vehicles. Army personnel had noticed that these were very effective in a variety of roles, especially that of gun tractor, and Bedford was asked to examine the vehicles in detail and come up with plans to produce something similar for the Allies.

In researching these, it seems clear that not a lot is known about the resultant vehicle as every source consulted trots out the same scant facts, some of them being almost word-perfect with what must be the original source, Vauxhall's own book, 'Account of our Stewardship', published in 1945-46, and written by W J Seymour. This being the case, it seems churlish not to give credit where credit is due and to quote the said author, verbatim.

'An outstanding item of German military equipment was the all-purpose 88mm gun, and one of its main features was its mobility. The Germans were able to move screens of these guns with great speed.

'The mobility of this gun was due in large part to the type of gun tractor employed. This tractor was the result of many years' intensive development, which had been started in secret even before Hitler came to power. The Germans had built and tested all known types of gun tractors, including four-wheel drive, six-

wheel drive, fully-tracked and semi-tracked vehicles. Their tests led them to the conclusion that the best vehicle for the purpose was the three-quarter track type. As the name implies, its tracks extend for approximately three-quarters of the length of the vehicle.

'The vehicle the enemy eventually developed was steered by the front wheels, and also by the tracks, both types of steering being controlled automatically by a normal steering wheel. On hard roads the vehicle steered like a normal wheeled vehicle, but if the front wheels were insufficient to provide adequate steering - in soft mud and so on - the track steering came into operation.

'There were many other very useful features, too technical to describe simply. Suffice it to say that, as gun tractors, these German vehicles were just about the last word.'

The account goes on to say that numbers of them were captured in Libya, and Vauxhall was asked by the Ministry of Supply to strip them down and prepare them for full military trials. They were then asked to design and develop a similar vehicle for the British Army to tow the 17-pounder, the 25-pounder and light anti-aircraft (AA) guns.

The latest types of German half-track vehicles were shipped to Luton and all available intelligence on their deficiencies was obtained from the War Office. In just over a

The 15cwt 4x2 MW, seen here with its original aero screens, was Bedford's first foray into producing military vehicles. (Vauxhall Motors)

The OX 30cwt continued to be produced throughout the War and was fitted with a variety of body types – seen here is a YMCA tea van. (Vauxhall Motors).

year Bedford had six prototypes running, designated 'BT' (Bedford Tractor). The general layout closely followed the German scheme, but with improvements introduced where they were known to be desirable. As the vehicles were very urgently required there was no time to design and develop a new engine of the necessary power, so two standard Bedford engines were used, side by side, geared together, thus saving time and simplifying the problem of supplying spare parts.

The six BT prototypes underwent thorough testing in 'mud and sand... in heat and cold and even in the sea' and were found satisfactory. The BT managed a gradient of 1:2, averaged 25mph on the road with a full load and gun, and achieved excellent average speeds by driving straight off the road, through ditches and over ploughed fields. It was made almost completely waterproof during production, and could be driven through six-foot deep water without affecting the engine or chassis.

Arrangements for large-scale production were well forward when VE day came and work was discontinued. It seems strange, if the BT really was such a remarkable vehicle, that the idea was not revived in the post-war years. The reasons for developing it were, after all, very different from those which led to the experiments with the QL-based 'Bedford Bren'

Bedford MW undergoing wading trials - some 5000 vehicles were treated for D-Day itself with a further 14,000 as follow-up. (Tank Museum)

half-track on which a Bren-gun carrier's running-gear was mated to a standard QL lorry. The idea emanated from an attempt to save raw materials but, unexpectedly, the outfit performed extraordinarily well, mainly because the QL had a driven front axle.

Quite apart from Luton's massive engineering output, a prodigious variety and quantity of drivers' and maintenance handbooks was produced, including a whole series in the Cyrillic alphabet for the USSR. Little booklets were written for drivers, in what was then considered a humorous style - but which would, today, be considered patronising. One such, entitled 'For BFs', contains useful tips for drivers - always aimed, of course, at 'the other fellow'. Examples include 'don't ride the clutch'; 'don't travel downhill in neutral' and, 'return the reserve tank switch to its normal operating position when you refuel', failure to do so inevitably resulting in the tank being run dry with no reserve - as the author, rather shame-facedly, found out for himself.

Bedford also founded the Bedford Drivers' Club, one of the earliest and longest lived of the one-marque clubs. This had its own magazine which, during the war years was reduced to a single page in the 'Commercial Motor' magazine. Amongst other features, this reported on where Vauxhall/Bedford training and service facilities were set up around the world - something which had to be discontinued when it was realised that it gave away almost every location in which British troops were operating!

Taken together, these activities built, for Vauxhall Motors, and, even more so, the Bedford marque, an enviable reputation for reliability

WATERPROOFING AND D-DAY CASUALTIES

During the planning for D-Day, it was clear that amphibious operations would require motor vehicles to be 'waterproofed' for off-loading from landing craft, enabling them to make their own way ashore through deep water. Waterproofing techniques were developed in great secrecy, and over a long period, but the desired results were eventually achieved using a compound commonly known as 'WD Plastic Putty' to encase the vulnerable electric components.

For wading, the specification required engines to be run, flat out, in bottom gear for several minutes in a considerable depth of water, and then to be capable of covering 200 miles on dry land immediately afterwards. For soft-skinned ('B') vehicles, this was described as 'no less than immersion in four feet of water, with eighteen inch waves for six minutes. For AFVs, the depth requirement was increased to six feet.

Some 5000 vehicles were treated for D-Day itself with a further 14,000 as follow-up and, in the event, 'casualties' were remarkably low, at less than 3%.

Examination of wading casualties on D-Day show that 1.5% were launched into deeper water than specified; 1.3% became bogged down or were lost by enemy action, and only 0.15% were lost due to poor waterproofing or bad driving: - a total of 2.95%. Vehicle casualty figures for the invasion itself are of interest. Statistics from REME for the period of the invasion show that, of the vehicles they were able to recover, battle losses accounted for only 2%. Mechanical failure accounted for 76% and vehicle modifications, a further 7% with - inexcusable, surely - lack of maintenance accounting for a shocking 4%. Finally, 11% of vehicles recovered had been involved in accidents. These statistics relate, of course, to vehicles of all makes, not just Bedford.

and innovation, not only with the various Ministries, but with drivers and fleet operators, something which was to stand them in good stead for the next 40 years. ■

BEDFORD ROUND-UP · 2

Robert Coates concludes his round-up of the story of Bedford military vehicles by looking at the years from 1945 to the present day

The still-born 6x6 FV1300 project was to be badged as 'Vauxhall' but there was never any series production; this is the FV1301 cargo truck - a crew-cabbed artillery tractor was also prototyped (FV1313). (IWM, MVE 25369/2)

Bedford's recovery from the 1939-45 war was rapid, with a return to production of 'normal' peacetime models - the K, M and O Types, which had been introduced in 1938 - before the end of 1945. By 1947, truck production had passed the half-million mark, about half of which had been military vehicles of one sort or another.

From 1951 onwards, the K, M and O models were superseded by the forward-control S, C and RL 'Big Bedfords' - in 1958, whilst these latter models were in production, the Luton firm's truck production passed the one-million mark. The 'Big Bedfords' were followed by the A, D and J Types which were so similar in many details that should really be regarded as three sub-types of the same range. In 1961 came the TK, and the rather-less successful face-lifted TL, as well as the MK and MJ military variants and the TM4-4 and 6-6. All of these Bedford models were supplied to the British armed forces, even if, in the dark days of 1939, many of them were simply requisitioned. Many overseas' armies also specified Bedford military vehicles, one of the Company's major assets having been its strength in export markets.

Bedford' were also major proponents of 'articulation' although this was more noticeable on the civilian side than the military, where the company had little or no influence on vehicle operations. To Bedford's way of thinking, articulation meant more than just having a vehicle which bent in the middle; it implied what is nowadays known as 'drop and pick-up' in which a tractor unit exchanges a loaded semi-trailer for an empty one, thus reducing turn-round time. Admittedly, the earlier QLC artic and OXC 'Queen Mary' trailers were articulated, but they fell outside this category as they were, to all intents and purposes, permanently coupled - with a Taskers of Andover ball-coupling. Most other types could, however, be separated, usually by means of the popular and widespread 'Scammell Automatic' coupling for which Bedford and Scammell had established a joint venture in which they produced articulated truck-and-trailer combinations, sold complete.

In this series of articles, which has followed the fortunes of Bedford military trucks, little has been said of military requirements for Bedford buses. Passenger chassis had featured in the Company's range from the earliest days and some of these chassis may well have been used by the military - certainly, the 1941 OWB 'utility' bus was pressed into military service. Mention should also be made of the articulated 'Bevin bus' with its 24-foot, 65-passenger trailer built by Dyson or the British Trailer Company and fitted out by Charles Roe. The name derived from the vehicle's use in transporting the 'Bevin Boys' - conscripted miners - to and from their place of work. After the War, production of the handsome OB bus resumed and, when the 7-ton S Type 'Big Bedford' was introduced, the range included a remarkably-successful bus/coach chassis designated SB. This was employed by the armed forces in various guises, including that of a large-capacity field ambulance in which the seats could be replaced by two tiers of stretchers. Bodies were produced by Duple, Plaxton and Strachans. Military buses were also produced on the 1961-69 VAS 30-seat chassis.

With the TK, Bedford's production passed the two-million mark, in 1969, and then three million in 1978 but, in 1975, the TM became the last truck range to be offered by Bedford under the ownership of General Motors - or by any of their successors for that matter. The Company called-in the receivers in 1986 and, although resuscitation attempts were made by AWD and then by Marshall's SPV, neither was successful. By the turn of the century, as a truck-producing company, the name Bedford had died, with only the spares organisation surviving.

Over the 55 years of their existence, Bedford produced, quite literally, millions of trucks, buses and vans - enough, in fact, to stretch some 11,500 miles if parked nose-to-tail. Along the way, their standard products have been modified for special purposes in a myriad ways - in both the civilian and military sectors.

One such was the RL 'coffin' - an armoured car, of sorts, which was used in Malaya in 1955-56. It was designed to be more-or-less mine-proof and the basis of the design was also carried forward on to the MK. There were two doors at the rear, squared-off wings with sufficient strength to carry the weight of people standing on them, and a triple armoured-glass window, about 3x5 inches, with a sliding piece. Neither the RL or MK versions looked anything like their parent vehicles and though they may have been extremely ugly, were spoken of with affection by those who used them.

In some ways, this RL/MK conversion may have been the precursor of the AT105 Saxon armoured car. Whilst not exactly a Bedford product, the GKN-produced Saxon armoured personnel carrier did incorporate a Bedford chassis and running gear, together with the famously-reliable Bedford 500 six-cylinder diesel engine of the TM 4-4 and 6-6 models. Produced by GKN Defence, the Saxon has been described as a 'battlefield taxi... designed around truck parts... thus not requiring the enormous maintenance of track and running gear normally associated with APC/AFVs'. It originated in the AT100-IS vehicle developed by GKN-Sankey in 1971 - this was not put into production, being superseded by the AT104 and then, in 1974, by the AT105. The first units were delivered to the British Army in 1983 and, although some 550 examples are in service, it was never considered as totally satisfactory. Even the Army handbook says 'as a vehicle capable of protecting infantry from shell splinters and machine gun fire in Europe during the Cold War years, Saxon was a useful addition to a formerly-larger Army. It does not, however, have the speed and agility which the lessons of recent mobile combat suggest will be necessary for

Military bus produced using the VAS2 chassis with 30-seat front-entrance body by Strachans; similar vehicles, constructed on the longer-wheelbase SB3 chassis, were convertible to the ambulance role.

Using the front-end mechanicals of a second-hand military M Type, with a new cab, axles and wheels, this prototype ultra-low-deck brewery dray used front-wheel drive to achieve its low height - it was not the eventual answer for ways were found to 'bend' the transmission sufficiently to retain rear-wheel drive. Some years later another attempt was made, mounting the engine back-to-front, with chain drive to the automatic gearbox and tiny wheels on the twin rear axles, the rear-most of which steered - unfortunately, it was a horrible thing to drive!

infantry to survive in the future'. In other words, this 'mine-proof' lorry - as distinct from an armored personnel carrier - has had its day.

The RL 'Coffin' has already been cited as an example but there were many others, from observation towers to runway sweepers, and an experimental tank transporter, Bedford's only foray into the really heavy end of the market. There are even

examples of Bedford military vehicles being modified for specialist civilian work, one such being the use of the front-wheel drive element of an MK to drive an ultra-low-deck brewer's dray. On this prototype, the load deck was too low to allow the transmission to be carried to the rear axle so it was reconfigured with front wheel drive.

Worthy of special mention, even though it never went into series production and didn't even carry the Bedford name was the FV1300 (see CMV, May 2003 issue). This was a Fighting Vehicle Design Department (FVDD) idea of the late-forties which hung around until the early to mid-fifties when Bedford came up with the RL. The FV1300 was to have been a purpose-built 6x6 military vehicle. It would have had little »

Bedford was always popular with export customers and the 4x4 RL was supplied to the Danish Army as CKD kits which were put together, with this local cab variation, by GM International A/S, Copenhagen. Known as the RLC5, there were cargo and shop body variants.
(Olle Willumsen)

The ambulance variant of the AT105 is capable of carrying four stretcher cases or a combination of stretcher cases and walking wounded. (GKN Defence)

In about 1988, AWD-Bedford produced this 75-ton 6x6 tank transporter. It was said to be suitable for a gross train weight of 120 tons and was powered by a Cummins NTE-400 turbo-charged diesel driving through a Fuller nine-speed gearbox. Sadly, there were no takers.

Taken in 'bandit country' in Malaya in 1956, with the Royal Regiment of Wales, this photograph brings a whole new meaning to 'off-road driving'. Using its own winch, the vehicle - which is an RL 'armoured coffin' - played a major part in its own rescue. Note that whilst it may have been mine-proof it was certainly not driver-proof.

or no appeal commercially and one can't help feeling that Bedford did not apply heart and soul to the project which, after a few - rather unsatisfactory - prototypes had been built, passed out of Vauxhall's hands. It was known, simply, as 'Truck, 3 ton (and also 6 ton), 6x6, CT, Vauxhall'.

What has happened to Bedford since 'going bust' in 1986.

After AWD and Marshall's SPV attempted to breathe life into the organisation, ERF acquired the remnants which, by that time, amounted to little more than the spares organisation. Jigs and dies were sold off, some even going to China and rumours of other deals abound. Marshall's produced TJs for Nigeria for a while and it is believed that production is to restart in, of all places, Ethiopia, using the dies formerly sold to China. MAN, of Germany, acquired ERF and then sold the spares organisation to Amethyst Logistics whom, it is hoped, will 'make a go' of supporting the thousands of Bedfords, both military and civilian, which are still in existence. Today, there are some 9000 British military Bedfords believed to be around with a similar number of 'civilians' in the UK most of the latter appearing in the form of horse-boxes, it seems. World-wide, the figure is thought to be around 160,000 still in service.

In the 'nineties, the British Army discovered that it was cost-effective to refurbish some of their ageing MJs, whilst 'casting' some of the much more recent Leyland DAF 4-tonne logistic support vehicles but this programme now seems to have been completed. Both MJs and TMs are, however, still in service and the TMs look like being there for a few years yet, whilst the Defence Procurement Agency makes up its mind about their replacement.

How sad that such a wonderful marque has now all but passed into history. Bedford might still be with us - and the whole UK truck-producing industry in a much healthier state - if it wasn't for those interfering politicians back in the 'eighties. Even so, the company has left behind it a rich heritage and, some might say, that Bedford has provided the all-time 'classic military vehicle'. **MILITARY**

The Bedford-derived GKN Saxon AT105 is the British Army's current wheeled armoured personnel carrier - it is not considered to be satisfactory for the current military situation. (GKN Defence)

Standard winch-equipped FV13105 3-ton truck as it appeared in military service - the photograph was taken on the FVRDE test slopes. This is an early vehicle with the 'high' headlight position.

Bedford RL conversions

L W Vass has been in the military-vehicle business for more than 60 years, concentrating on finding new careers for 'one-owner' military vehicles

MILITARY-VEHICLE enthusiasts of long-standing will probably need no introduction to the Ampthill-based company of L W Vass Limited. Although it has tended to concentrate more on finding new commercial careers for ex-military vehicles, rather than catering for the enthusiast, the company has been in the military-surplus market for going on 60 years and has also been a useful source of parts for those in the know. One of the company's specialities was the re-bodying or conversion of military vehicles to make them more suitable for civilian life. For example, quite a few of the AEC Matador-based recovery vehicles which were mentioned in these pages a few months ago had their origins in the Bedfordshire yard of 'Lawrie Vass'.

In the early 'seventies when the Bedford MK was starting to replace the RL, large numbers of surplus RLs from war reserve and Home Office Auxiliary Fire Service (AFS) stocks were being released through the Ministry auctions at Ruddington. Although these were generally older vehicles, the mileage was often very low and their condition was such that they were eminently suitable for civilian applications, either in the developing world where roads were perhaps not up to the standards of Europe, or in domestic applications where the four-wheel drive system would be an advantage.

And, of course, the RL already had a civilian counterpart which meant that the vehicle was familiar to many operators.

Despite its conservative 3-ton rating, the military 4x4 Bedford RL was actually based very closely on the 7-ton 'S Type' civilian chassis - the so-called 'Big Bedford' - which had been launched in 1950. The modern, no-nonsense 'S Type' featured a straight-through chassis frame of generous dimensions, and was available in a choice of wheelbase lengths 116in, 132in and 156in, with a short-chassis tractor, of 86in, also produced for use with semi-trailers; most military vehicles featured either the 132in or the longer, 156in, wheelbase.

Telehoist SL54 twin-ram tipper conversion.

Converted chassis with shorter, 126 in³, wheelbase and twin rear wheels.

The engine was front-mounted in the forward-control configuration - in fact, the 'S Type' was the first civilian Bedford to be offered with forward control - and, depending on your point of view, was fitted with what could be described as a stylishly-curved, or hideously-bulbous, almost-three seater cab. The flat, two-piece windscreen had a distinctive shallow 'V' shape.

On both the military and civilian vehicles, power was initially derived from Bedford's all-new, seven-bearing six-cylinder petrol engine of 4927cc (300in³) producing 110bhp at 3200rpm and 234 lbf/ft of torque at 1200rpm.

Although a diesel engine was eventually offered to the civilian market, it did not find favour with the military until the introduction of the MK in 1970 and the RL continued to employ the original petrol engine. On the rear-wheel drive civilian vehicles, the drive was carried through a single dry-plate clutch of 12in diameter, to a unit-mounted 4F1R transmission. The four-wheel drive military vehicles had a lower final-drive ratio and the standard four-speed gearbox was supplemented by a two-speed transfer case which gave selectable front-wheel drive.

Following the usual period of testing, the 4x4 RL was accepted into military service in 1952, remaining in production until 1969. Altogether 73,135 examples were constructed during this 17-year period, giving an average number of vehicles per year of almost 4500. A similar, but slightly 'value-engineered' (isn't that what it's called these days), four-wheel drive chassis was also made available to civilian purchasers in 1953.

In just a few short years the 'S Type' had established itself as a favourite with civilian operators in the medium-weight class, being both reliable and comfortable. To quote the Company's own words, the 'Big Bedford' was literally 'seen everywhere' - there was even a related bus chassis. It was hardly a surprise then, that when surplus RLs became available, L W Vass considered them to be prime candidates for conversion to various civilian roles. And, of course, they knew that there was a ready-made market.

Steel tanker conversion.

A series of attractive brochures was produced showing vehicles which had been fitted with various types of standard body including an Edbro or Telehoist all-steel 5 or 6yd³ tipper body with twin-ram hydraulic tipping gear, 800-gallon steel tanker for fuel or water, and an Atkinson 5yd³ grit or lime spreader - some 300 of which had been supplied to local authorities up and down the country, with a number even finding their way to the Transvaal in South Africa. Other roles described included a medium-recovery vehicle using a 6-ton Harvey Frost crane - a similar 3-ton version was also available on the FV1601 Humber chassis - and a cargo truck with Hiab hydraulic loading crane.

In those distant days when labour costs were comparatively low, Vass ran a big operation, employing a workforce of around 100 men. This meant that there was always sufficient time to steam-clean the vehicles thoroughly, to strip the chassis and cab and to check all components thoroughly, replacing any worn parts before the thing was put back together and sent away for re-bodying. Key sub-assemblies such as the axles and transmission were actually taken right down to their component parts on the bench, and bearings, oil seals and shafts were replaced with new parts wherever wear or damage was evident. Engines were stripped and reconditioned. Unless a customer had specified twin rear wheels, the original three-piece wheels were retained, and a set of good 11.00x20 bar-grips - or 'snow-grips' as they were described on the grit spreader - was fitted. All vehicles were supplied with a

new battery... and if the military green paint was not suitable, the customer could also specify a choice of colour for a modest additional sum.

The price of the renovated chassis-cab was £600, which compared very favourably with the price of £780 for the long-wheelbase chassis-cab at the time of its launch in 1950. An 800-gallon tanker could be fitted for £400 and a Telehoist tipping body for £480. A twin rear-wheel conversion, using a new axle with a lower ratio, cost £180, and the thirsty petrol engine could be replaced by a reconditioned Bedford 330 diesel for £265. And if the chassis was not entirely suitable for a customer's projected use, Vass offered a conversion to a shorter 126in wheelbase for £65. There was also a range of other options, including heavy-duty rear springs, cab heater, and flashing amber beacon, making the vehicles suitable for a variety of roles. The high degree of commonality between the 'S Type' and the RL also meant that the company was able to supply ex-MoD spares for both models at a considerable discount on the manufacturer's list price.

Clearly the standard of work was very high for, over a 20-year period, Vass tells me that literally thousands

of these reconditioned chassis were supplied to customers all over the world.

L W Vass are still in the military-vehicle business and, are still at Station Road, Ampthill, Bedfordshire. The business remains much the same with a mix of civilian and overseas military customers, with the odd enthusiast hoping that some older trucks or parts are lurking in the back of the yard. Current stock includes ex-MoD Land Rovers and larger trucks, and a good number of interesting fire appliances. The company continues to specialise in Bedford parts - although of course these days the parts are for more modern types - and also has literally tons of parts for 90in and 110in Land Rovers. They can be contacted on 01525 403255 or check out 'www.vass.co.uk'

Surplus RLs were once a very common sight at auction and at the larger dealers in ex-military equipment. Here's a couple of ex-AFS vehicles, the left-hand one an RLC chassis equipped with a decidedly non-military steel body, the other an older RL with the Home Office timber general-purpose body.

Fire Goddess

Aleister Crowley, amongst others, described absinthe as the 'Green Goddess' - we are more concerned here with those topical, but ancient, fire appliances

AM I alone in being irritated by that smug media phrase 'ageing Army Green Goddess fire engines'? OK, admittedly, they are green and they are certainly ageing, but they do not belong to the Army, nor even the Ministry of Defence! The military connection is simply that they are crewed by Army personnel.

But having got that off my chest, since the Goddesses are very much in the news - at least at the time of writing - we thought it might be educational to take a closer look at them.

The so-called Green Goddesses were purchased by the Home Office for civil defence use back in the early 'fifties and, since 1 April 2002 have been owned by the Office of the Deputy Prime Minister. Collectively, these anachronistic vehicles are described as the 'emergency reserve fleet' and, although there has not been a national firemen's strike since the nine-week long dispute in 1977, the Goddesses are frequently deployed to provide fire cover during local disputes, notably in Liverpool last year. As well as deputising for strike-bound fire appliances, they can also be loaned out to local authorities, to assist in pumping operations during severe floods. The vehicles are stored at RAF Marchington where, for a number of years they were maintained by a civilian organisation - TNT TruckCare - but the maintenance has now gone back in-

Green Goddess exhibited at Eden Camp in North Yorkshire.

Des Penny

house, where it always used to be. Same mechanics - different paymaster.

More than 3500 of these vehicles were built between 1953 and 1956 on a standard Bedford truck chassis. Some 1400 early examples were constructed on the twin rear-wheeled 4x2 S Type chassis and were given the designation SHZ,

whilst the majority - more than 2000 - which were designated RLH, were constructed on the 4x4 RL chassis; both used the standard 156in wheelbase. The vehicle was not actually conceived for use as a civilian fire appliance, but was purpose-designed to deal with various civil-defence incidents; in fact, the standard Green Goddess is correctly described simply as a 'pump, self-propelled' or as an 'emergency pump' (E/P). Typical roles included the provision of a relay pumping system for water, for example for drinking purposes, or for decontaminating streets in the event of a nuclear attack. The basic formula for use as a relay pump was to provide one pump vehicle every half-mile on level ground; on inclines, the distance between pumps was reduced. The vehicle could also be used as a fire pump, either using its on-board water supply or by picking up water from a hydrant, or open supply.

The Goddess is well-equipped for its role as a relay pump by virtue of the powerful Sigmund FN4 single-stage,

Steve Crampton

Previously assigned to the AFS at Huntingdon, this SHZ Goddess shows off the body storage lockers; note the 'fire bell' on the cab roof.

Army Fire Service Goddesses were usually painted red rather than green.

Technical specification

Nomenclature: pump, self-propelled, 4x4 or 4x2; Bedford RLHZ, SHZ.

Engine: Bedford; six cylinders; 4900cc; overhead valves; power output, 95bhp at 3000rpm; torque, 234 lbf/ft at 1200rpm.
Transmission: 4F1R; 4x2 or part-time 4x4.
Suspension: live axles on semi-elliptical leaf springs.
Brakes: hydraulic.
Construction: steel ladder chassis with pressed-steel cab and timber-framed steel-panelled body.
Electrical system: 12V.

Dimensions
Length, 276in; width, 89in; height, 126in (RLHZ 4x4 with ladder in place). Wheelbase, 156in.
Weight, 18,000 lb laden (RLHZ 4x4).

With a fire strike looming, during the last few weeks soldiers have been training with Green Goddesses.

engine-driven pump which is capable of feeding four hose-lines with 900 gallons per minute at a delivery pressure of 100lbf/in²; the pump is driven from the transfer box and is rated for continuous duty. Standard on-board equipment includes 1800 feet of 2¾in rubber-lined delivery hose, in 100-foot or 75-foot sections, with instantaneous couplings; each vehicle also carries four 8-foot lengths of 5in suction hose. A 300-gallon 'first-aid' water tank is mounted in the centre of the chassis, which can be used as an alternative to supply from a hydrant, etc. The system is also capable of producing foam when necessary. A Coventry-Climax lightweight portable pump is carried in a locker immediately behind the cab; the pump is mounted in a cradle which allows it to be slid down to the ground for ease of use. Fire-fighting equipment includes 360 feet of ¾in reinforced-rubber hose carried on hose-reels mounted on either side of

the body, a two-section 35-foot aluminium-alloy ladder, plus a range of other tools and equipment.

Visually, the Goddess is a surprisingly handsome machine with a purposeful air to it - but there again, beauty, as ever, is in the eye of the beholder! The distinctive bulbous RL front panel/scuttle, with the special flat two-piece windscreen developed for this application, works much better than it has any right to when combined with a very plain and angular six-man crew-cab body. Folding access doors are fitted on either side of the body behind the front wheels, and there were all manner of lockers to allow the vehicle to carry the equipment deemed necessary for its envisaged role. The bodies were built by a variety of companies including Papworth Industries, Thomas Harrington,

Weymann, Plaxton, Park Royal Vehicles, Strachans (Successors), Windover, and Willowbrook.

At the time of their manufacture, the vehicles were under the control of the Home Office and were issued to local authority Auxiliary Fire Sevice (AFS) units to supplement the 'red' appliances. A small number of almost identical vehicles was also purchased by the Army Fire Service and, aside from being painted red, these can be recognised by the presence of an additional locker behind the near-side rear wheel.

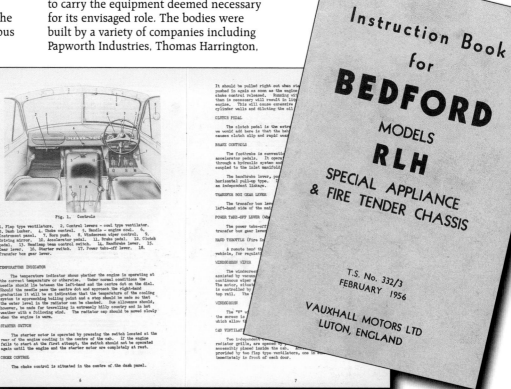

Operation

In the event of industrial action by civilian fire-fighters, personnel from all three of the Armed Forces have been trained and prepared to provide basic emergency cover.

When standing-in for a conventional fire appliance, the Green Goddess is manned by a crew of six services personnel. These include a driver, who has undergone a special Green Goddess course to master the handling of the vehicle, and a non-commissioned officer who is trained to act as crew commander.

The Green Goddess crews are trained to fight and contain fires and, clearly, their highest priority is to save human life. To this end, two types of dedicated rescue teams, formed from professional Royal Air Force and Royal Navy firefighters and other military personnel who have undergone an intensive five-week course, are available to back up the Green Goddess crews. The three-man 'breathing apparatus rescue teams' (BARTs) are trained and equipped for the dangerous task of entering a smoke-filled building, as well as dealing with road-traffic accidents. Where more specialised equipment or skills are needed, 'rescue equipment support teams' (RESTs) are also on hand. The BARTs and RESTs deploy in modern vans, fitted with blue lights and appropriate markings. Like the Green Goddesses, these vehicles will receive a police escort when responding to an emergency, and the drivers have undergone 'blue light' driver training.

Up to 827 Green Goddesses, manned by 10,000 personnel from all three of the Armed Forces, are available if needed. 331 BART teams have been trained, along with 59 REST teams: these comprise a further 2500 personnel.

Some 6500 other personnel are also available to support the operation.

Steve Crampton

Side elevation view shows the contrast between the distinctively-rounded Bedford nose and the plain, flat-sided body.

Both the vehicle chassis and the pump equipment were chosen for ease of operation by relatively-unskilled personnel.

Despite unkind comments to the contrary, the vehicle is perfectly capable of speeds up to 50mph but, perhaps, the road-holding is not all that one might expect at the beginning of the 21st Century. The high centre of gravity, particularly when carrying 300 gallons of water, has led to several vehicles overturning when used at speed on normal roads.

Those which remain in service are exclusively of the all-wheel drive variety - the 4x2 machines having been disposed of within a few years of the winding-up of the AFS and Civil Defence organsiations in 1968... and for what it's worth, the all-wheel drive feature actually gives the Goddess a better cross-country capability than a standard fire appliance. The

vehicles are well maintained and there is no evidence of the unreliability which has been suggested by certain elements of the press.

Surplus Goddesses are disposed of from time to time, but around 900 remain in store, and a recent major exercise saw most of these fitted with a diesel engine in place of the original Bedford petrol unit. Nevertheless, the Goddess has the dubious honour of being the oldest working fire appliances in the western world.

At the time of writing, there is every possibility that the Goddesses will, once again, be a familiar sight in our towns and cities - and whilst it might not be for the best of reasons, we should be thankful they were never called on to keep the streets clear of radioactive dust...

...but why were they were nicknamed 'Green Goddesses'?

Edward Angus

The red high-visibility stripe and the blue light on the roof are recent additions, otherwise this Goddess is just as it left the bodybuilders almost 50 years ago.

THE ONE THAT GOT AWAY!

It seems that Vauxhall's 6x6 FV1300 prototypes were a rare example of an unsuccessful Bedford military vehicle

Although there is just a hint of the Bedford RL about it, the FV1300 was by no means a handsome beast. (IWM, MVE 19580/5)

Bearing in mind the 60-year contribution that Bedford made to the development of British military vehicles, it is a little surprising to learn of an area in which the Company not only failed, but also, effectively, had a military contract terminated and passed to a rival manufacturer. The vehicle in question was the advanced 6x6 FV1300 series - and perhaps that use of the word 'advanced' explains the problem. Bedford's military output had tended to concentrate on vehicles which made a virtue of sound, no-nonsense engineering. The basic design of the FV1300 was a product of the Fighting Vehicle Design Department (FVDD) and their approach was somewhat at odds with Bedford's own thinking.

The 6x6 FV1300 series was intended to provide the 3-ton component of the British post-war 'combat' vehicles range, of which the FV1800 Austin Champ formed the bottom end and the 60-ton FV1000 formed the top. These so-called 'CT' vehicles were defined by the War Office as 'specialised military vehicles with multi-wheel drive, manufactured from components not used for commercial purposes, and required to give the best possible load-carrying capacity and cross-country performance, with or without the appropriate guns or trailers'. The 'CT' family included vehicles in the standardised weight classes ¼ ton, 1 ton, 3 tons, 10 tons, 30 tons and 60 tons. The basic design principles were laid down by FVDD and there was a very high degree of commonality in approach across the weight classes. Although the two largest vehicles, the FV1000 and the FV1200, were to be powered by the Rover V12 Meteorite engine, others shared engines from the Rolls-Royce 'B Range', and there were also other areas of similarity, for example, the ¼-ton, 1-ton and 3-ton vehicles all featured independent suspension by torsion bars.

In 1947, FVDD and the War Office had

drawn-up the plan which defined these six classes of vehicle. It was very much a reaction to the multiplicity of vehicle types for which the British Army found itself trying to provide maintenance and parts support during WW2, and although the plan was basically rational, it foundered utterly on two counts. Both of these are well illustrated by the failure of the FV1300 project.

The first problem was one of practicality. FVDD maintained that its experiences with commercial vehicle manufacturers during the war years demonstrated that the latter had little understanding of the particular requirements for the design of military vehicles. This may well have been true, but what was equally true was that FVDD had no idea of how to design for production, neither was the organisation able to draw on the near 50 years' experience of motor vehicle design which was available from the industry.

The second problem was cost. Even if it had worked, to design every component for a range of specialised vehicles from scratch would have been prohibitively expensive.... and, the fact that it did not work, for the reasons outlined above, served only to increase the costs still further.

But, we are, as they say, getting ahead of ourselves.

It was originally intended that the

FV1313 artillery tractor undergoing towing trials with the FV2841A 3-ton trailer loaded with a Class 30 bridging pontoon. (IWM, MVE 22721/4)

and the long-wheelbase FV1301 3-ton GS cargo vehicle, which would have replaced the Bedford QL.

The specification for the artillery tractor, issued in May 1948, stated that it was intended to cope with a towed load of 45cwt together with two ammunition trailers, each of 30cwt. Maximum speed on good roads was to be 45mph - no maximum speed across country was specified, but the document contained a slightly curious statement regarding a minimum speed of $2\frac{1}{2}$mph which the vehicle was to be able to maintain 'over long periods without overheating'. The body was to accommodate a crew of six together with a spare gun wheel and essential stores - in design, it was required to be 'inconspicuous' with a height not

The production body for the cargo vehicle - seen here fitted to prototype number 7 - was a fixed-sided design in steel. (IWM, MVE 25369/2)

FV1300 series would include specialised vehicles for the cargo, artillery tractor, signals, recovery, telephone/radar repair, and ambulance roles; early lists produced by FVDD showed no less than 17 variants. Even before detailed design work was undertaken, budget considerations dictated that the range be simplified and only the cargo, artillery tractor and recovery variants were commissioned for development. The range was subsequently further simplified when the recovery tractor was also removed from the equation.

So, by the time the War Office actually started to commission work, the range consisted only of the short-wheelbase FV1313 crew-cabbed medium artillery tractor - intended to replace both the Morris Quad FAT and, in some roles, the AEC Matador gun tractor of WW2 vintage -

exceeding 102in. There was to be belly protection against anti-personnel and HE mines containing up to 20 lb of

explosive. The rest of the specification was pretty standard stuff and most details were shared with the cargo vehicle, but it was stated that the vehicle was to 'be capable of the easiest possible conversion from right- to left-hand drive'.

In 1949, nine prototypes were ordered from Vauxhall Motors Limited for delivery at the end of 1950; two were artillery tractors, the remainder were cargo vehicles.

It is easy to understand why the project was placed with Vauxhall Motors - after all, as has been spelled out in the introduction, their Bedford trucks subsidiary had done such sterling work during WW2 producing the 4x4 QL, the 15cwt MW, the various models in the O Series, and so on. Quite why the FV1300 was described as being a 'Vauxhall' - a name which was not generally used for trucks - rather than 'Bedford', remains something of a mystery, but at least it helped to avoid undue tarnishing of Bedford's reputation when the project went belly-up!

The vehicle was powered by a Rolls-Royce B80 Mk 1D eight-cylinder engine producing 165bhp from a capacity of 5675cc. Drive was transmitted through a dry-plate clutch to a three-speed plus reverse gearbox,

Test body fitted to the crew-cabbed artillery tractor. (IWM, MVE 20581/6)

together with a two-speed transfer case; in common with other vehicles of the period, such as the Champ and Ferret, all of the gears were available in both forward and reverse. »»

(IWM, MVE 25318/9)

Prototype number 1 was delivered in 1951 and took the form of the FV1301 3-ton cargo vehicle - seen here with a timber test body. (IWM, MVE 19580/3)

Suspension was independent at all wheels. There were lateral torsion bars at the front, whilst the rear bogie consisted of a conventional single axle driving a complex arrangement of four walking beams suspended on torsion bars. Interestingly, even after the project was terminated, Vauxhall continued to develop this suspension and in November 1952, the 'Commercial Motor' magazine reported that the Company had patented (patent number 678580) this arrangement using laminated leaf springs in place of the torsion bars... although it doesn't seem to have been used in any other vehicles.

To say that the bodywork was curiously styled would be an understatement.

The radiator grille was strongly horizontal whilst the cab was rather upright and, somehow, this contrived to give the vehicle a sad, droopy look that was entirely at odds with its purpose. The crew cab of the artillery tractor had two doors on either side, hung from the 'A' and 'C' posts, respectively; both cabs were provided with twin circular hatches in the roof for an anti-aircraft gun. The rear body of the FV1301 cargo vehicle was of steel construction and was provided with the usual hoops to support a canvas tilt, whilst the rear body of the artillery tractor was of timber, with a centre partition. None of the sheet metalwork was shared with other Bedford vehicles, and there is a weight of evidence to suggest that it was not actually constructed by Vauxhall at all but may well have been built by Mulliners.

Almost immediately, questions were raised regarding the vehicle's reliability.

As soon as the trials began, there were problems, the most notable being a weakness in the chassis which led to cracking during cross-country work. The vehicle was described in a War Office as being 'inordinately complicated' and of '...giving every indication of problems to come'. One writer said that there were so many problems apparent with the vehicle that it was unlikely that it would ever be satisfactory.

At the same time, the cost issue reared its ugly head, with the average price of the production vehicles estimated at £5500 each. This price was based on a production quantity of a staggering 20,000 vehicles but this was later cut to just 3000, and then to 1000. Inevitably, the reduction in quantity caused the price to rise - by 1953 it was up to £6875, which is more than £170,000 in today's money. The Director General Fighting Vehicles (DGFV) promised ≫

FV1313 artillery tractor photographed during trials at Bagshot. (IWM, 24940/3)

'LIES, DAMNED LIES AND STATISTICS' – 1

In a detailed coda to his splendid Bedford series, Robert Coates starts to summarise the production of what was once Britain's classic military vehicle

Military 30cwt W-Type with oversized tyres – note the typical military vehicle wheels.

The oft-misused quotation, 'Lies, damned lies and statistics', is normally attributed to David Lloyd-George who thus revealed, at a stroke, how politicians misuse and abuse a noble science. However, he was not the only one and there are many 'anti-statistician' quotations - 'he uses statistics as a drunk uses a lamp-post: more for support than illumination' and 'he frequently used 'bikini' statistics: what they revealed was interesting but what they concealed was vital', are just a couple of examples. Yet it cannot be denied that some statistics are interesting, revealing and often give hitherto unforeseen insights to familiar topics.

It is in this spirit that the following attempt has been made to produce tables of statistics relating to the production, from cradle to grave, of what was probably Britain's greatest-ever truck producer. 'You saw them everywhere' and they all carried the Bedford badge - over three and a half million of them.

These tables, arranged a decade at a time, have been compiled from numerous sources, some more reliable than others. There are many gaps and many inconsistencies and it is hoped that, rather than criticise and 'pull them to bits' readers will supply authenticated corrections so that a true, or perhaps truer, picture can be built up.

Throughout the tables, a dash against a particular model in a particular year indicates that the model was not produced during that year whilst an 'n/a' signifies that it was produced in that year but that no detailed breakdown has been found.

1931-39

Vauxhall Motors started producing trucks - or lorries, as they were usually called in those days (and still are by traditionalists) - in 1931. Prior to that they had assembled imported Chevrolets which, over the years, had progressively incorporated a larger and larger proportion of 'home-produced' components. Yet there was still market resistance to 'foreign' lorries and Vauxhall, a wholly-owned subsidiary of General Motors of America, decided to introduce an all-new British variant to combat this. Casting round for a name which sounded

Next month we'll start to look at the war-time production – typified by these OXC tractors with Scammell trailers. (IWM, H29184)

suitably British, they came up with Bedford: it was purely fortuitous that, some years later, production was moved form north London to Luton, in Bedfordshire. It was also coincidental that those of their vans which had load-space above the cab, became known as 'Lutons'. These, in common with similar vans made by other manufacturers, took their name from the old stage coaches in which there was a compartment where passengers could store their tall hats. As hats were, at the time, one of the major outputs of the town of Luton, the compartments became known as Luton-heads. (Not a lot of people know that!)

One of the earliest 'Bedford' military vehicles – not shown in the tables – was actually a Vauxhall D-Type touring car. (Vauxhall Motors)

For the first decade, 1931-39 - which, of course is only nine years - figures for each model have been extracted from hand-written records from the (Vauxhall) Engineering Records Department, held at the National Motor Museum, at Beaulieu. These are probably as reliable as any, but discrepancies can occur between 'plan' and 'actual' and with different period ends.

The breakdown between models of the W Type production were extracted from 'Centre Section' (number 76), the magazine of the Bedford Owners' Club, where they had been reproduced, having first been published in 'Old Motor', volume 11, number 3. They are probably from ex-factory records. Frustratingly, the totals (some of which are from a different source, thought to be equally reliable) do not always coincide with the sum of the numbers shown but, as it is not known which are the more reliable, both sets of figures are reproduced.

It is also worth pointing out that the 30 cwt Chevrolet truck accounted for 6254, 5047 and 284 vehicles for 1930, 1931 and 1932, respectively whilst the 12 cwt Chevrolet van sold 866 units in 1930 and 977 in 1931 with production ceasing in 1932 after 70 vehicles had been made.

As the figures show, the new long- and short-wheelbase 2-tonners, introduced In 1931, with the long- and short-wheelbase buses and new 30 cwt WS added in 1932, took the market by storm. The new

BEDFORD PRODUCTION, 1931-39

Years ending 30 September

	1931	1932	1933	1934	1935	1936	1937	1938	1939	Total
WH, WHG 2 ton	1503	2649	2651	2698	2258	2468	2938	1643	-	18808
WLG 2 ton	3326	3948	7274	5908	5128	6406	8443	4965	-	45398
WS 30 cwt	261	2409	3563	3083	4090	4400	5775	3422	-	27003
WHB 14 seat	36	54	14	-	-	-	-	-	-	101
WLB 20 seat	338	473	489	369	224	-	-	-	-	1890
WTH 3 ton	-	-	-	668	1731	1643	2196	1411	-	7659
WTL 3 ton	-	-	-	1903	7017	6051	6971	4682	-	26624
WTB 26 seater	-	-	-	-	655	945	643	-	2243	
Total W Types*	5463	8530	13090	14630	20452	21628	27273	21655	14402	
ASYC, 12 hp	-	-	626	1197	1228	1169	1273	885	439	
ASXC, 14 hp	-	-	181	738	438	721	1188	927	417	
BYC, 12 cwt	-	-	-	350	1166	2250	1646	1096	810	
BXC, 12 cwt	-	-	-	286	457	442	403	402	256	
VYC	-	1288	500	491	-	-	-	-	-	
VXC	-	357	776	131	-	-	-	-	-	
HC, 5 cwt	-	-	-	-	-	-	-	2509	1861	
Total Bedford	7120	11487	10529	15173	17823	23741	26210	31783	27474	18185

*The totals shown are derived from separate sources and do not necessarily tally with the individual year-by-year model totals.

The Bedford MW first appeared at War Office trials in 1936 although it didn't go into production immediately – note the civilian vehicles surrounding the MWs.

Bedfords, which were simple, rugged, good looking and good value for money were launched the same year as Standard-Swallow decided to name their cars 'SS Jaguar', a car which was also simple, rugged, good-looking and good value for money. Both also had smooth-running, 'straight-six' engines.

The WT model, introduced in 1934, was to set the design standard for lorries right up to the time that 'forward control' became the fashion. The essence of the change was that the engine was placed above the front axle, rather than behind it giving improved ride and manoeuvrability and a useful increase in load space for a given length of vehicle. Some operators even fitted bus and coach bodies onto the WTL chassis to take advantage of these characteristics. By 1939, we have some additional detail about the WT: chassis numbers in this year ran from 5886 to 20287 and engine numbers from 6949 to 21281, a total of 14,333 engines representing a 'spares ratio' of about 5%, cumulatively. Production of the W Type ceased in 1939 with a total of 147,123 vehicles having been made.

As for light vans, the total for the V Type was 3543 of which just over 64% were VYCs, and for the AS type, 11,427 vehicles of which just under 60% were ASYCs. The B Type total was 9564 of which 7318 were BYCs.

In addition to the totals shown, production of Vauxhall's H range, which included model HC (a van variant), amounted to 16,898 vehicles in 1938 and 15,857 in 1939. The K, M and O models, and the Bedford-Scammell, were introduced in June 1939, but more-or-less immediately suspended for war production.

Apart from prototypes, no models were shown as having been produced specifically for the armed forces during this decade but Vauxhall's financial year ended in September, so this is a little misleading: production in the last calendar quarter was recorded as 1940 financial year's production. Next month we'll start to examine war-time production. **Military**

...to be continued

Impressed 2-ton W-Type serving as a make-shift troop transport vehicle. (Tank Museum)

'LIES, DAMNED STATISTICS' – 2

In a detailed coda to his splendid Bedford series, Robert Coates continues to summarise production of what is almost certainly Britain's classic military vehicle, this month looking at the years 1940-49

Nearly 66,000 of the 15-cwt MW were constructed during the War years – the open cab and aero screens are typical of the early production. (Vauxhall Motors)

Last month we examined Bedford's pre-war production record... this month we turn our attention to those, oh-so important, 'forties, during which Bedford produced more than 400,000 trucks and vans.

Throughout the tables, a dash against a particular model in a particular year indicates that the model was not produced, whilst 'n/a' signifies that it was produced in that year but that no detail breakdown has been found.

1940-49

This decade is dominated by the war years, for which records seem to be quite good. Most of the figures have been extracted from Bedford's ERD (Engineering Records Department) documents held at the National Motor Museum, Beaulieu. These figures usually agree with data published by Bedford in 1945, which quotes chassis and engine numbers, and so are thought to be reliable. There are, though, some important exceptions probably due to different period ends, double counting, or differences between manufacture and issue. For example, ML models of 1940 are quite probably included in the ERD figure for K, M and O models since the ERD would not have been concerned with what body was fitted.

The predominant war-time models were the MW 15 cwt, the OY 3-tonner and the OX which was available as a 30 cwt rigid or as a 6 ton artic tractor, all of which had the characteristic squared-off front of war-time Bedfords. There was also the 4x4 forward control QL and the A22 'heavy vehicle', better known as the Churchill tank.

The figures for model HC, for 1940, (chassis numbers 5371-7212) include 192 model J1, six-cylinder, 14HP, produced for the RAF. Figures from ERD for the K, M and O models show some interesting discrepancies with those derived from chassis number records, for which I can offer no explanation. Similarly, the figures from the ERD for the 'A22 heavy vehicle' are known to be wrong since only 5640 Churchills were built. However, the phasing may be correct so the 'true' figure has been re-cast, pro-rata, to the ERD phasing. The overall discrepancy is too small to account for the 'out-working' or 'parenting' which Bedford carried out with other Churchill manufacturers.

The detail for the forward-control QL 4x4 is extracted from my book 'Bedford to Berlin' - now, sadly out of print - which deals exclusively with this model (apart from comparisons with other manufacturers' contemporary offerings in the same class). Year totals are known to be correct and model totals are, in some cases, known and, in others, have been extracted from the original contract cards which are held at the Tank Museum, Bovington. Where discrepancies occurred, the gaps have been filled by 'forensic arithmetic'.

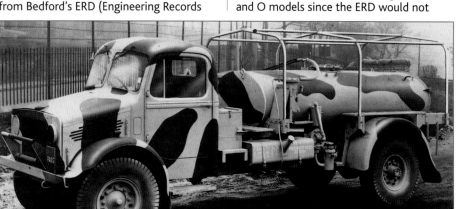

Bedford OYC 3-ton water tanker – some 72,000 examples of the OY were built between 1939 and 1945. (Vauxhall Motors)

30-cwt Bedford MSC with a standard RAF cargo body by Spurlings. (Vauxhall Motors)

A hand-written annotation on the back of this photograph suggests that it was taken at Spurlings premises – it shows war-surplus QLs, OYs and MWs.

For the years 1948 onwards, the Bedford total agrees with figures compiled independently by the SMMT (Society of Motor Manufacturers and Traders); other years were either simply not compiled by them or have found an unknown home. Amongst the SMMT figures is an interesting breakdown showing, for a number of manufacturers as well as Bedford, production by various classes. Taking as a (more-or-less) random sample, December 1948, production - or, possibly, registrations - in that month, for Bedford, were as follows:

- *vehicles under 15 cwt, 665*
- *vehicles 15 cwt to 6 tons, 2657*
- *PSV, 163*

PSV (public service vehicles) includes trolleybuses, but this was one class in which Bedford did not compete. Whilst the figures, on their own, are fairly meaningless, they do give an indication of how records were kept at the time, as well as indicating Bedford's participation in each class. In percentage terms, 76% of Bedford's output was in the 15 cwt to 6 tons category - they produced nothing at that time over 6 tons, this class being dominated by the likes of Leyland, Albion, AEC and several others; 19% of their output was in the under 15 cwt category - mainly light vans - and the remaining 5% was of PSVs, all of which would have been OBs - not bad for a single month although, by that time Bedford enjoyed the lion's share of the bus and coach market with this model. The famous OB was, in fact, not just the predominant Bedford PSV during this whole decade, but the predominant British - and, probably, world - PSV, many thousands of them having been produced post-war.

At the foot of the table are three rows of 'Totals', one from ERD and the other

BEDFORD PRODUCTION, 1940-49
Years ending 30 September

	1940	1941	1942	1943	1944	1945	1946	1947	1948	1949	Total
HC 5/6 cwt van	1842	-	-	-	-	-	1364	1703	1357	-	
JC 10/12 cwt van	2940	-	-	-	-	-	2276	3552	3745	n/a	
PC									1165	6950	
K, M, O (ERD)	9856	-	-	-	-	52	25442	26647	28025	n/a	
OS, OL, OB	n/a	-	-	-	-	5150	27000	19992	28025	30085	
ML54 ambulance	397	-	-	-	-	-	-	-	-	-	
ML55 tanker	45	-	-	-	-	-	-	-	-	-	45
OWS, OWL, OWB	-	1644	7418	6715	6057	10757	-	-	-	-	
MW 15 cwt	14440	13965	13746	14666	4270	4908	-	-	-	-	65995
OX 30 cwt, 6 ton	9976	5393	2280	2308	2388	2083	-	-	-	-	24428
OY 3 ton	15100	15078	13557	12516	9356	6777	-	-	-	-	72384
QLB	-	1269	774	1859	816	782	-	-	-	-	5500
QLC	-	1914	2347	902	404	1374	-	-	-	-	6941
QLD	3	2224	4446	6666	7318	5047	-	-	-	-	25704
QLR	-	766	2174	2406	1698	1739	-	-	-	-	8783
QLT	-	54	1191	346	1545	237	-	-	-	-	3373
QLW	-	-	-	-	-	1947	-	-	-	-	1947
(Total QL 4x4 3 ton	3	6227	10932	12179	11781	11126	-	-	-	-	52248)
(A22 'heavy vehicle')	5	1110	2187	2166	1617	-	-	-	-	-	7085)
'Corrected total', A22	4	884	1741	1724	1287	-	-	-	-	-	5640
TOTALS											
ERD	52749	40983	48948	50814	35741	38773	29084	32002	34292	n/a	
This table	52762	43417	49674	50108	35139	40853	29082	31902	34292	37035	
'Discrepancy'	13	(566)	(274)	(706)	(602)	2080	(2)	(100)	0	0	
TOTAL BEDFORD	**54696**	**39873**	**46761**	**48648**	**34124**	**38773**	**33809**	**31077**	**35522**	**38144**	

obtained from various sources. The discrepancies, which cannot be accounted for, are noted but the net discrepancy across all the years is only 157 vehicles. This can possibly be accounted for in the 1949 figure for which no known ERD figure exists. In any case, published figures from Bedford, also shown, are available and these are believed to be accurate; the other series are shown for interest and to illustrate the difficulty of arriving at what might be considered as reliable figures. MILITARY

Early OXD 30-cwt general service truck.

'LIES, DAMNED STATISTICS' – 3

In a detailed coda to his splendid Bedford series, Robert Coates continues to summarise production of what is almost certainly Britain's classic military vehicle, this month looking at the decades of the 'fifties and 'sixties

The S Type was also pressed into military service, this RAF bulk refueler is constructed on a militarised SLC chassis.

The SB coach chassis was used by both the Army and the RAF as a dual-purpose coach/ambulance (39 seats/16 stretchers) – although Duple was the coachbuilder of choice for most civilian customers, these military ambulances were generally constructed by Strachans

Last month we examined Bedford's war-time production record... this month we turn our attention to the 'fifties and 'sixties during which Bedford firmly established itself as Britain's leading producer of light and medium trucks.

Throughout the tables, a dash against a particular model in a particular year indicates that the model was not produced, whilst 'n/a' signifies that it was produced in that year but that no detail breakdown has been found.

1950-59
This decade covers the post-war period, the 'export-or-die' era in which home demand had to take a back seat to exports. Once the K, M and O models had been discontinued, new models were introduced thick and fast, starting with the so-called 'Big Bedford' (the S Type and its four-wheel drive military counterpart, the RL), a '30 mph 7-tonner' which was rapidly followed by the A, D and J Types. The records for these seem to be excellent.

The figures in the table have been built-up from month-by-month production records (in various conditions and states of repair) which show the first chassis number off the line each month. As in previous tables, the model totals are for this decade only.

For the K, M and O models as a whole, one source quotes total production as being 412,000 of all types, but no breakdown is available and the figures are not substantiated. Another source states that the 'all-time' total build for these models is 262,289 vehicles, most of which probably went for export - another example of how difficult it is to establish the true picture; they could well both be right but looking at different markets (eg, 'total home' and 'total all' markets).

The 1950 figure for the O models, albeit substantiated by chassis number records, is

LIES AND

obviously much higher than previous or subsequent years, but no figure was available for this model for 1949 so perhaps this represents two-years' production.

In 1955 the company moved truck production to Dunstable and, in 1958, Bedford produced their millionth vehicle.

1960-69

This decade was certainly the 'swinging sixties' for Bedford who turned in some colossal annual production figures. Unfortunately, so far as this exercise goes, a new method of record-keeping was introduced in 1965-66 and most of our hitherto fascinating detail is lost, absorbed into an unfathomable 'Total Dunstable trucks'.

Two lines operated at Dunstable, a fast one and a slow one and, by 1970 we have the additional information of the numbers produced on each line, but no detail of which models were involved: it is not even possible to ascertain whether 'Dunstable trucks' includes passenger chassis. As previously, model totals, where shown, are for this decade only. Annual totals, of unknown reliability, are available for 1960-64, being 113,857 for 1960; 89,931 for 1961; 74,525 for 1962; 134,267 for 1963 and 136,946 for 1964: thereafter figures are too unreliable to include here, especially as it is not known precisely - if at all - which models are 'in' and which are excluded.

For the RL, in 1965, the figure shown is for January to June only, any later production being included with 'Dunstable trucks'. The 1965 figure for the CAS and CAL models is an estimate compiled from various sources. After 1965, the records are so unreliable as to be not worth including; indeed some of the CA production may have been included with Vauxhall car production which is outside the scope of this exercise.

Probably Bedford's greatest model ever was the TK and it is a pity that the data from halfway through this decade are incomplete. The figure for 1961 is part actual, part 'educated guesswork'. The January to November figure (actual) is 21,745; the guesswork applies to the December figure.

It seems probable that passenger chassis totals are included in the 'Dunstable trucks' total as these were hybrid lines, successive vehicles capable of being entirely different models as is the modern practice, in which virtually every vehicle is built to order and to its own individual specification.

The SB passenger chassis was available throughout the decade and could be seen with many body variants at home and abroad. Duple provided the majority of

coach bodies for the home market but there were others, too. The VAS model, a 29/30-seater bus/coach with petrol or diesel engine options, was available from 1961, being discontinued in 1969. It was joined by the VAL twin-steer 55-seater in 1962 and this model ran through to 1972. The VAM 41-45 seater ran from 1966 to 1970.

In 1969 Bedford produced their two millionth vehicle, of which 1,500,000 had been trucks. **MILITARY**

Derived from the so-called 'Big Bedford' of 1951, the RL was, without doubt, 'the' Bedford military vehicle of the 'fifties and 'sixties, with more than 50,000 examples constructed.

BEDFORD PRODUCTION, 1950-59

Years ending 30 September

	1950	1951	1952	1953	1954	1955	1956	1957	1958	1959	Total
PC	10384	8555	3258	-	-	-	-	-	-	-	30312
CA	-	-	3248	9858	14268	17445	19872	21038	21435	24835	137481
CAL, CAS	-	-	-	-	-	-	-	-	-	-	5482
K, M, O	78749	26134	26816	10482	-	-	-	-	-	-	142181
S (inc SB)	-	4579	7444	11,977	8584	8119	8562	7533	8028	7654	72480
RL	-	-	2114	3784	4070	4277	5527	5067	2353	3370	30562
C	-	-	-	-	-	-	-	1159	1306	734	3133
A	-	-	-	14551	28916	29172	35319	6927	-	-	114885
D	-	-	-	-	-	-	-	14494	23443	-	37937
D (other source)	-	-	-	-	-	-	-	14820	22934	-	37764
TJ	-	-	-	-	-	-	-	-	-	29850	29850
Totals:											
Table	89133	39268	42880	50652	55838	59013	69280	56544	56056	71925	
Bedford	40783	43382	42969	48445	57556	67933	63226	58783	55439	88720	

1960-69

Years ending 30 September

	1960	1961	1962	1963	1964	1965	1966	1967	1968	1969	Total
CAL, CAS	40823	24921	18908	71105	58626	29282	-	-	-	-	
CF	-	-	-	-	-	-	-	-	-	n/a	
S (to Jul 60)	-	8219	-	-	-	-	-	-	-	-	8219
RL	3690	2448	2083	3603	5179	3882	n/a	n/a	n/a	n/a	
C	457	-	-	-	-	-	-	-	-	-	457
JO	263	1268	679	571	2226	251	-	-	-	-	5258
TJ	52019	37794	29976	30642	36127	19728	n/a	n/a	n/a	n/a	
TK	8386	23500	22879	28346	34788	21080	n/a	n/a	n/a	n/a	
KM	-	-	-	-	-	-	-	n/a	n/a	n/a	
'Dunstable Trucks' - not recorded as such before Aug 1965						33465	71376	45999	35921	37706	
Totals:											
Bedford	106284	94595	76661	84798	106672	113825	101898	89296	97925	101821	

'LIES, DAMNED STATISTICS' – 4

In a detailed coda to his splendid Bedford series, Robert Coates looks at the final decades of Bedford production, finishing with the 'seventies and 'eighties.

In the early 'eighties, the MK was joined in service by the TM 4-4 and the larger TM 6-6. (Vauxhall Motors Limited)

Last month we examined Bedford's production during the 'fifties and 'sixties. In this final instalment we look at the 'seventies and the disastrous 'eighties which heralded the end of Bedford production as we know it.

Throughout the tables, a dash against a particular model in a particular year indicates that the model was not produced, whilst 'n/a' signifies that it was produced in that year but that no detailed breakdown has been found.

1970-79

Information on individual models, apart from the newly introduced, and largely unsuccessful, TM, are virtually non-existent for this decade. All we have to go on is the total numbers of vehicles produced on the 'fast' and 'slow' lines at Dunstable. As can be seen, times were becoming less buoyant, with the fast line producing, in a bad year, only a few more vehicles than the slow line in a good one. For example 11,446 'fast line' trucks were produced in 1979, against 11,232 from the 'slow line' in 1972. However, by mid-year 1978, the 500,000th TK had been produced (in Portugal), and by the year end, the millionth Bedford van and the two-millionth Bedford truck had been built.

As for passenger models, the by now ageing SB was still going strong (it was eventually discontinued in 1980). New Y models became available: the YRQ 45-seater - Bedford's first mid-engine under-floor coach chassis - was around until 1975 when it was replaced by the YLQ, 45-seater which ran from 1975 onwards. There was also, from 1973-75 only, the YRT, a 53-seater, and a new model, the JJL which was introduced in 1977.

1980... TO THE BITTER END

This is a tragic decade - the one in which Bedford, as part of General Motors, 'went to the wall'. World truck demand was a fraction of what it had been; foreign imports were accounting for the lion's share of what little there was of the British market; exports were difficult because of exchange rates and there was massive political interference in the automotive industry. The outcome is revealed all too clearly in the figures. The TK's pitiful replacement in 1980, the TL with its non-tilting cab, and the TM with its very unpopular V6 two-stroke engine

The civilian TK chassis was also pressed into service with both the Royal Navy and the Army, albeit in slightly militarised form. Note the typical frontal position for the exhaust pipe on this 6x4 fuel tanker. (Vauxhall Motors Limited)

Flat-bed MK equipped with a communications shelter.

which was replaced by more conventional machinery too late to affect the eventual outcome, were available, as were the last gasps of the M range. The slow line at Dunstable eventually shut down in 1981.

'Official' figures for 'Total Bedford' peter out in 1983 and even that year is comprised of part actual, part forecast. The figures for 1987 and 1988, which relate to the interim period during which the receivers were 'in' and production

Derived from the civilian TK, the 3-ton 4x4 MK and the subsequent MJ, remain the British Army's workhorse to this day, having only been partly superseded in service by the later 4-tonne Leyland-DAF.

was, eventually, transferred to AWD's control, are of unknown reliability having been extracted from hand-written notes on the bottom of some old production

record sheets. The last Bedford vehicle, ex-conveyor, was JT102023 on 26 February 1988; the first AWD vehicle ex-conveyor was JT 200101 and the first (AWD) model for the 1989 model year was KT200101 on 28 July 1988.

Was this, then, the end? For truck production - yes, pretty much so. For the Bedford name? Not quite - Marshall's SPV eventually acquired limited rights to use of the name on certain vehicles in certain markets. The name lives on today, as Bedford Genuine Parts under the aegis of the Amethyst Logistics organisation. Long may it do so to service the 160,000 Bedfords still believed to be operating world-wide, which includes 16,000 in the UK of which the Ministry of Defence have some 9000 due to be finally phased out in 2014. For the older vehicles - those in preservation of one kind or another - the market will, we hope, continue to be serviced by such organisations as Bygone Bedford Bits who have the breadth of experience of pre-1950 vehicles which is required in the enthusiast market. MILITARY

BEDFORD PRODUCTION 1970-79

Years ending 30 September

	1970	1971	1972	1973	1974	1975	1976	1977	1978	1979
Model availability - trucks:										
TJ	n/a	n/a	n/a	n/a	n/a	n/a	-	-	-	-
TK	n/a	n/a	n/a	n/a	n/a	n/a	n/a	n/a	n/a	n/a
KM	n/a	n/a	n/a	n/a	n/a	n/a	n/a	n/a	n/a	n/a
M	n/a	n/a	n/a	n/a	n/a	n/a	n/a	n/a	n/a	n/a
TM	-	-	-	-	-	-	-	-	-	n/a
Dunstable Trucks:										
'Fast line'	21068	23148	17387	16142	15896	17289	19551	16350	18622	11446
'Slow line'	8435	11232	7673	7804	8580	8799	8149	6962	10406	5877
Total Dunstable	29503	34380	25060	23946	24476	26086	27700	23312	29028	17323
TM line (start-up)	x	x	x	x	x	x	x	x	x	29
Total Bedford	101660	91053	112151	86390	117443	126394	107257	91311	91747	87650

1980-88

Years ending 30 September

	1980	1981	1982	1983	1984	1985	1986	1987	1988
TK	n/a	-	-	-	-	-	-	-	-
TL	n/a	n/a	n/a	n/a	n/a	n/a	n/a	n/a	n/a
KM	n/a	n/a	n/a	n/a	n/a	n/a	-	-	-
M	n/a	n/a	n/a	n/a	n/a	n/a	n/a	n/a	n/a
TM	n/a	n/a	n/a	n/a	n/a	n/a	n/a	n/a	n/a
Dunstable Trucks:									
'Fast line'	12409	6612	9820	10204	10816	10750	6249	3482	2704
'Slow line'	6587	1783	-	-	-	-	-	-	-
Total Dunstable									
TM Line	1441	1488	1286	790	839	580			
Totals									
This table	20437	9883	11106	10994	11655	11330	6249	6964	2704
Total Bedford	94219	48211	51734	52898	n/a	n/a	n/a	n/a	n/a

The AWD-Bedford ML was derived from the earlier MK/MJ models. (AWD Limited)

The German origins of the rear tracks are very obvious in this view but you can hardly describe it as a handsome machine - this is prototype number 6. (IWM, MVE 9554/6)

TRACLAT

The editor looks at the Bedford Traclat - a curious Anglo-German hybrid design which was intended for use as an artillery tractor but which never went into production

Although the British had experimented with Citroën-Kégresse, Crossley and Burford-Kégresse half-tracks between the Wars, and received large numbers of US M3/M5 half-tracks during WW2, there were no home-grown half-tracks put into series production. The key word here is 'production' because attempts were made during WW2 to construct a British half-track. For example, the Ministry of Supply (MoS) constructed a half-track 3-ton truck by replacing the rear wheels of a standard Bedford QL with a shortened track assembly from a Bren Gun Carrier and submitted this to the Wheeled Vehicle Experimental Establishment (WVEE) for trials. A similar experiment was made with an AEC Matador and, although neither went into production, these were not the only such vehicles of this type to be constructed in the UK.

The best known is probably the Bedford Traclat.

The Traclat - 'tracked light artillery tractor' - came about when, in 1943, the MoS asked Vauxhall Motors to construct a three-quarter tracked artillery prime mover which used a similar track and rear-suspension system to that of a captured German 8-ton Sd.Kfz.7 medium

artillery tractor. The Sd.Kfz.7 had been developed by Krauss-Maffei in the mid-thirties to tow 10cm and 15cm guns.

The first stage in the project involved shipping a number of German half-tracks, which had been captured in Libya, back to Britain and asking Morris-Commercial Cars - or more likely, Nuffield Mechanizations - to put them

through a trials and evaluation programme with a view to developing a similar machine for British use. By early 1945, Vauxhall Motors had been contracted to construct six prototypes of what it subsequently described as the 'BT' - or Bedford tractor - but which the Army dubbed the Traclat.

It was envisaged that the Traclat would be used as a towing vehicle for the 17- and 25-pounder field guns and for the Bofors anti-aircraft gun. The British Army had been impressed by the performance of the German tracked gun tractors in North Africa, and it was hoped that the wheeled/tracked driveline would provide improved mobility when compared to the existing wheeled vehicles which the British were using for »

The radiator grille, which protected twin radiators, was distinctly Jeep-like. (IWM, MVE 9554/5)

The body was divided into three separate areas - cab, ammunition and equipment stowage, and gun crew - each of which could be dismounted separately. This is prototype number 2. (IWM, MVE 9554/7)

this role.

Aside from the three-quarter tracks, which were a virtual copy of those used on the Sd.Kfz.7, the most interesting feature of this machine was the power unit... or rather, power units. In the absence of the time or resources to develop a suitable engine, Vauxhall elected to install a pair of six-cylinder overhead-valve truck engines side by side under the bonnet. The two engines, which were similar to those installed in the ubiquitous Bedford QL, produced a combined 136bhp from their 3519cc each, albeit with a combined fuel consumption scarcely better than 3.5mpg (1.27km/litre).

The drive from the two engines - each of which, incidentally, had its own cooling system and radiator - was taken to a transfer/collector box at the back of the gearbox, by means of separate propeller shafts, and then the combined drive was passed back through a standard clutch to the five-speed main gearbox. Although the output from the engines was coupled together in this way, in an emergency, it was possible to drive the vehicle on just one engine. The gearbox also incorporated a Cletrac controlled-differential unit which both transmitted the drive to the front sprockets and also controlled the steering action of the tracks. Normal steering action was effected through the front wheels but when the steering wheel was turned beyond half of its lock, the differential was brought into the equation giving a minimum

Rear view showing the winch rollers beneath the body. (IWM, MVE 9554/7)

turning circle of 50 feet (15.25m).

Following the principles established by German vehicles of this type, the front axle was suspended on a single transverse leaf spring, whilst the double bogie wheels at the rear were suspended on transverse torsion bars. The tracks consisted of steel castings with rubber pad inserts, linked through oil-filled needle roller bearings - the life of the pads was in the order of 2000 miles (3200km) but it was said that Vauxhall had considerable difficulty with the design of the rubber pads.

Maximum road speed was governed to 30mph (48km/h) but the tracks gave the vehicle a much higher average speed cross-country than could be achieved with a wheeled gun tractor and it was perfectly capable of maintaining its maximum speed with a towed load on a 1:30 gradient. The vehicle could also tow a 25-pounder up a gradient of 1:2.

A wide bonnet was required to cover the two engines and, combined with the open cab and upright, folding windscreen, this contrived to make it look rather like a Bedford MW on steroids. The radiator grille had six vertical slots in the style of the WW2 Jeep. Most photographs show rounded front mudguards but, in his excellent - but sadly, long out-of-print - book 'A Kaleidoscope of Bedford and Vauxhall Military Vehicles', Bart Vanderveen suggested that some of the prototypes also had Jeep-like flat mudguards.

The cab provided seating for a driver and one passenger on separate seats whilst, at the rear, there was an all-steel body consisting of two separate enclosed compartments. The five-man crew was accommodated on bench seats in the rear section, whilst the centre section, which had dropsides, housed the spare wheel as well as providing a stowage area for ammunition and equipment. There were anti-aircraft hip rings attached to the supports for the full-

Rear view of prototype 6 showing the twin anti-aircraft gun positions and the entrance to the gun crew area of the body. (IWM, MVE 9554/9)

length tilt, one above the passenger seat in the cab and the other on the right-hand side of the centre section.

It would be fair to say that it was a homely rather than handsome machine and, inevitably, from certain angles it looked rather German which might have caused some identification problems in the field.

There was a 5-ton mechanical winch installed under the chassis which could be used to pull forwards or to the rear, and there were pintle hooks front and rear, the latter being designed to swivel through 90° in either direction, which was intended to help with manoeuvring the gun into position.

Official trials were set up at the Fighting Vehicle Proving Establishment (FVPE) in July 1946. The vehicle was required to tow the 25-pounder gun and

Unusual rear towing pintle was designed to swivel; note the Jeep-like trailer socket at bottom left. (IWM, MVE 9554/4)

limber, and was pitched against a Crusader artillery tractor, which was derived from the obsolete Crusader tank, and an Alecto self-propelled gun, which of course was derived from the Harry Hopkins light tank and was never really intended for use as a gun tractor. Of the ≫

In the absence of a suitable large power unit, the Traclat was equipped with a pair of Bedford truck engines. (IWM, MVE 9554/7)

three, it seems that the Traclat gave the best performance but, since this was the role for which it had been designed and, anyway, it had been developed from a very successful German machine of the same type, that shouldn't be a surprise... and it seems that the performance of the tracks was not sufficient to prevent the vehicle from getting thoroughly bogged down in some particularly muddy ground.

Although a number of the machines were shipped to Germany where the trials continued, the project almost certainly came to nought because of excessive cost, and there was no series production. One of the prototypes saw civilian service with a forestry company on logging duties.

This was not quite the end of the project, for the post-war plan for a range of standardised British military vehicles included 8/10-ton three-quarter tracked medium and heavy artillery tractors, load carriers, ambulances, etc using a similar chassis. These were designated FV800 and FV900 but, as far as is known, none was constructed and it remains the case that there were no production British half- or three-quarter tracked vehicles. **MILITARY**

This, heavily retouched, photograph came via the Vauxhall-Bedford historic collection and appears to show a Traclat prototype on trial. (Vauxhall Motors plc)

OK... there never was a commercial Bedford QL tanker... but there could have been... and Brian Veale has the pictures to prove that it would have worked

Twin-boom refueller on the chassis of an RAF QL tanker (post-war registration, 10AD50); a sticker on the cab front indicates that the tank is 'Gas Free' which, presumably, means that it was steamed out prior to sale.

Way back in the mists of time, Brian Veale was a motor engineer with Shell-Mex and BP Limited, and in 1957, became involved in a special conversion of some 20 surplus Bedford QLs which were destined to act as plant-refuelling tenders during the construction of the M1 motorway.

Several trips were made to the Ministry of Supply auction sales at Ruddington to select suitable candidate vehicles for conversion and, eventually, 20 QLC-based fuel tankers were chosen which were in good all-round condition and which had already been overhauled by the Army or recently fitted with reconditioned engines. All of the vehicles were driven straight from Ruddington to the Shell-Mex BP central workshops in Fulham where the conversion work was to be carried out.

The photographs show the extent of the work that was required to adapt the trucks for their new role of refuelling plant away from surfaced roads.

Since the vehicles which were purchased had been constructed as fuel tankers, the original tanker body was retained, but new access ladders and catwalks were fitted; cab fire-screens were already in place which meant that there were no problems with gaining compliance with the necessary regulations. The original six-cylinder Bedford engines and pumping equipment were considered to be perfectly adequate for the job but new Zwicky metering equipment was installed. Racks were fitted to either side of the vehicle to carry dispensing containers. And, of course, they were refinished in the distinctive red and yellow livery of the Shell-Mex company.

The conversion work was carried out by W P Butterfield who had been manufacturing tankers for a number of years.

Although the vehicles initially gave good service, as the M1 contract progressed and the terrain became more difficult, there were a number of chassis failures. Later vehicles were constructed on the Bedford RL chassis, initially using ex-Army stock, but subsequently using new vehicles.

CIVVY STREET

Above and below: The completed tanker. Note the added catwalks and access ladder, can stowage racks and spotlight on the cab roof.

Close-up of the Zwicky metering equipment, using a Brodie-Kent flow meter; the display shows that the pump has delivered a total of 93.1 gallons.

However, these were not the only QLs that Shell-Mex BP had used for this type of work. The introductory photograph to the article shows a lone QL with twin-boom refuelling equipment which was also constructed for the M1 project. This carried a Coventry-Climax flat-twin engine in the pumping compartment at the rear.

A total of 52,250 Bedford QLs were constructed between 1941 and 1945 - this is the QLR communications variant. (Steve Crampton)

BEDFORD QL

Despite being Bedford's first foray into all-wheel drive, the QL was an enormously successful truck, with many examples clocking-up as many miles in civvy street as they did in military service.

Most of those constructed were the QLD 3-ton cargo vehicle, but there was also a troop carrier (QLT), signals vehicle (QLR), tipper (QLW) and Bofors gun tractor (QLB); the QLC was a chassis-cab intended for specialist bodywork and it was this chassis which was used for the construction of the refuellers.

Power was provided by a six-cylinder overhead-valve petrol engine producing 72bhp from a capacity of 3519cc, driving both axles through a four-speed gearbox and two-speed transfer case with front-axle disconnect. Live axles, front and rear, were suspended on semi-elliptical multi-leaf springs and the hydraulic brakes had vacuum-servo assistance.

The vehicle was in production from 1941 until 1945 with a total of 52,250 trucks manufactured.

M1 MOTORWAY

It should perhaps have been called the M5 or M6 since that's the way it goes, but clearly the planners couldn't resist naming Britain's first 'proper' motorway as 'M1'. In truth, it wasn't even the UK's first stretch of motorway - this honour goes to the Preston By-Pass which had opened the previous year.

The first section of the M1, which comprised 72 miles of dual-carriageway, 132 bridges and 32 culverts, was opened on 2 November 1959 by the Rt Hon Ernest Marples MP, the then Minister of Transport and Aviation. The work cost £16.5 million, which worked out at £270,000 per mile in rural areas and £2 million in the urban areas; by the time it was completed, the road had cost a total of £50 million.

Construction of this first section, which ran from St Albans in Hertfordshire to Crick in Northamptonshire, had taken just 19 months - this gives an average construction rate of one mile every eight days! Some 5000 men were employed, using £5 million worth of machinery, and caravan camps were provided for the workers who, even today, stay on site during the working week - one of these was located at the former prisoner-of-war camp at Sherington, near Milton Keynes.

Despite Marples describing it as 'a magnificent motorway opening up a new era in road travel, in-keeping with the new, exciting, scientific age in which we live', the road opened with no speed limits, no lighting and no central crash barriers... but at least the traffic kept moving!

The road was designed by Sir Owen Williams and Partners, and John Laing & Son Limited.

GREAT DANES

The editor examines the curiously-cabbed Bedford Rls supplied to the Danish Army in the 'fifties

Design and development of the 4x4 3-ton Bedford RL began in December 1950, with the vehicle entering production in April 1952. The RL was based on the 7-ton civilian S Type - the so-called 'Big Bedford' - and was intended as a replacement for the Bedford QL and other WW2 three-tonners such as the Austin K5 and Ford WOT6.

The reverse-slope of the windscreen gives a very strange appearance inside the cab. (Ole Willumsen)

Danish RL in its as-delivered guise; note the US style steel cargo body.

Line-up of RLs awaiting restoration. (Ole Willumsen)

Powered by a six-cylinder overhead-valve petrol engine producing 130bhp from 4927cc, the RL employed a four-speed gearbox and two-speed transfer case. The chassis was thoroughly conventional, with live axles suspended on semi-elliptical springs, but the combination of plenty of torque and excellent frame flexibility gave the vehicle a creditable off-road performance.

The RL was extremely successful, quickly becoming the British Army's standard workhorse and going on to serve with the armies of Belgium, Ireland, Malaysia, the Netherlands, Pakistan, South Africa... and Denmark.

In 1956, the Danish Army ordered a batch of left-hand drive RLC5 chassis-cabs through GM International in Copenhagen, arranging for them to be fitted with locally-produced upper-cabs and bodies. The distinctive Danish cab was notable for its large circular roof hatch with a conical canvas cover, and the reverse-slope windscreen, which gave it a rather 'beetle-browed' appearance but which, presumably, was intended to minimise reflections... or perhaps it was because the rather small roof of the standard RL cab was unable to accept the huge American-style anti-aircraft ring mount which was mounted on the chassis behind the cab. As regards load-carrying facilities, the Danish Army rejected the FVRDE-pattern drop-side cargo bodies specified for British vehicles, in favour of a fixed-sided steel cargo/troop-carrier body patterned on that fitted to US Army post-war 'deuces'.

The Danish RL became the standard load carrier in its class and, as well as the 3-ton cargo bodies, other variants included command and control vehicles, office van, telephone switchboard, teletype, shop van, and track layer. As with the British Army RLs, some chassis were fitted with a 5-ton under-chassis winch - these were designated RLW.

A second batch of approximately 375 units was

purchased between 1963 and 1967.

In 1968, the RL was uprated to 4-ton capacity and by the time production was terminated in 1969, more than 73,100 examples had been produced. In both British and Danish service it was replaced by the Bedford MK/MJ, with the Danish Army taking delivery of 250 MK chassis in 'knocked-down' form in 1972.

Thanks to Ole Willumsen of the Danish Historic Military Vehicle Association. For additional information; visit 'www.dmkf.dk'.